ROSSNAGALLIAGH

A COUNTRY SCHOOL

1839-1977

ISBN 978-0-9572398-0-7

Published by NDAHS 2012
www.newbuildingshistorical.org.uk

Printed by Browne Printers Ltd, Letterkenny
tel. +353 (0) 74 9121387

CONTENTS

FOREWORD

I was delighted to be asked by Ruth to write the foreword to this history of Rossnagalliagh – A Country School 1839 - 1977. Through her collaborative efforts involving members of the local community, and with the support of the local Historical Society and The Honourable The Irish Society, she has played a critical role in putting on public record the Community's collective memory of the past: a memory which might otherwise be lost to future generations.

This book makes an important contribution to our understanding of 19th century education in Ireland. It goes beyond a mere description of the curriculum and the teaching styles which characterised the 19th and 20th century primary school education to challenge our thinking about schooling. In the opening decade of the 21st century there has been a great deal of discussion about the educational policies linked to a shared future and how we move forward from a system that is largely shaped by sectarian considerations. The history of Rossnagalliagh reconnects us to a shared past where a local community accepted and promoted 'integrated education' in an organic, pragmatic sense rather than it being a product of an imposed policy.

The narrative of this country school's development challenges us to learn from our history as we try to rethink the future. It has important lessons to teach us. Perhaps if other local histories were explored in a similar way, a more informative dialogue between past and present could be ignited. This book makes an excellent start on that journey of discovery and the author is to be commended for her contribution to the debate.

Anne Heaslett

Dr Anne Heaslett
Principal
Stranmillis Univeristy College
Belfast

ACKNOWLEDGEMENTS

The decision to write the history of Rossnagalliagh School was taken when some of the school's early 20th century roll books and daily reports were kindly lent to me by Paddy Flanagan, a former pupil, and teacher in St Columba's Primary School in Newbuildings. Roll books from the 1960's and 1970's were also made available from St Columba's archives. The assistance of staff from the Public Records Office in Belfast helped point me in the direction of a variety of archives connected with the School, including inspector's reports.

The book was envisaged as a collaboration with those who attended Rossnagalliagh, and as a result I am indebted to the many past pupils and teachers who gave of their time to attend meetings, gave interviews and photographs, or helped with names and addresses, all of which helped preserve particular memories of the school. Their contributions can be found throughout the book.

Over the period of writing the book I have been supported by fellow members of Newbuildings & District Archaeological & Historical Society. The committee, in particular, have been invaluable in reading the script for publication. I am also very grateful for the Society's considerable contribution to the funding of the publication and to the book launch, and their decision to include the book among its publications. Special thanks to Paul Haslam and Roger Mccorkell for their time and expertise.

The Honourable The Irish Society agreement to also part fund the book is very much appreciated. The Society played an important part in the life of Rossnagalliagh School and I am grateful to Edward Montgomery, their representative in the area, for his assistance.

Many thanks also to my mentor and friend, Dr Anne Heaslett, who kindly read the script and agreed to write a preface to the book. Her encouragement, as always, was invaluable.

Finally, during the writing and production of the book, family and friends have been very generous in their support and encouragement. I am particularly grateful to my husband, Derek and son, Ross for unfailing help with many aspects of the book.

The school was situated on the main Londonderry to Strabane road

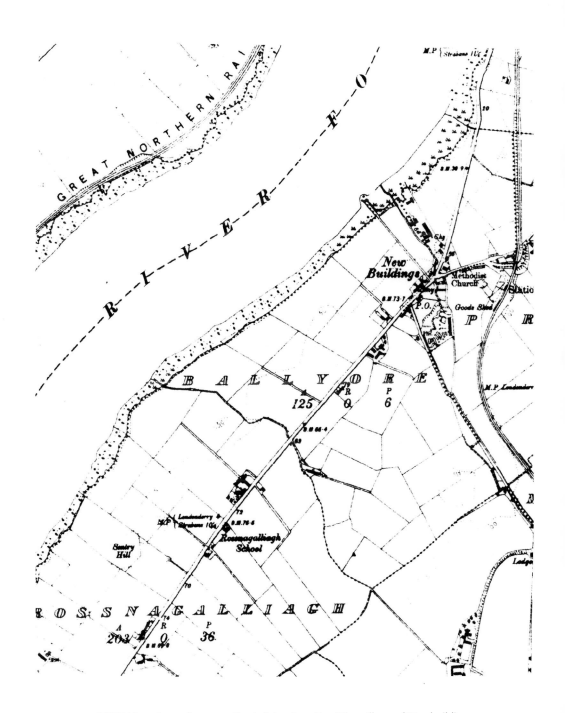

1907 Map shows Rossnagalliagh School south of the village of Newbuildings.

Most of the children attending Rossnagalliagh came from the above townlands.

INTRODUCTION

Rossnagalliagh School was to be one of the many national schools in Ireland which enabled local children to gain a free primary education. The school provided not only for children in Rossnagalliagh and the nearby village of Newbuildings, but townlands north towards the Waterside area of Londonderry and south into Co Tryone. (see townlands map)

Although the school was to come under the auspices of the Roman Catholic Church, it was to welcome children of all denominations until 1950's, while most national schools in Ireland were eventually lopsided towards one denomination by 1900. The successful integration of local children at primary level for over a century, therefore, is one of the most important reasons to investigate and record the history of Rossnagalliagh.

CHAPTER 1

PRIMARY EDUCATION AT PARISH AND LOCAL LEVEL

Throughout Ireland, by 1824, there were approximately 10,400 day schools with around half a million pupils being educated at primary level. A commission of inquiry believed that this was around two fifths of the children of school age. Many of the schools, however, were of inferior quality, with minimum equipment and in highly unsuitable surroundings. For example, in Curryfree, the school was described as a "thatched hovel" and Killymallaght School was held in "the loft of a barn".(See townland map) [1]

Setting up the Board of Commissioners for National Education in 1831, under a Government grant of £30,000, was an attempt to end these problems, as well as to provide "combined moral and literary and separate religious education". As a result some 2,500 schools were built in Ulster between 1832 and 1870. [2]

In comparison, as late as May 1839, there were still debates in Westminster around the subject of national education in England. Post Union Ireland was therefore to be treated differently from other parts of the United Kingdom, being the first to set up a National Education Board under the Executive in Dublin.

In the whole Parish of Clondermot, where the townland of Rossnagalliagh was situated, not more than 80 children were shown in the 1821 census to be in education but by1824 there were 678 pupils in 20 schools.

A decade later in 1834, 836 pupils were being taught by 16 teachers in 14 schools, between the ages of 5 and 15.

However Colonel Colby, who was part of an Ordnance Survey team in the Parish, wrote,

"Children of the lower orders but rarely spend the whole period from 5 to 15 under instruction, many indeed, but a small portion of it. It is possible that if only half their number be found at any one time at school, the whole may nevertheless receive the advantage of elementary instruction" .[3]

There was to be quite a lot of debate on the subject of full time primary education at this time, as can be seen in the Londonderry Standard in May 1839, when a correspondent wrote,

"A current mistake in society is due to the belief that the whole duty of the parent, so far as respects education, is discharged by sending children regularly to school. I should not hesitate to attribute greater importance to home education than school education".[4]

Nevertheless, those who produced the Ordnance Survey of the Parish commentated "indeed so strong is the desire for education that a woman has been known to keep her children at school for some time after the death of her husband had obliged her to beg for their subsistence". [5]

The death of the father such as this in a cottier family, where the children had not reached a mature age, would have meant an end to wages coming in. Therefore the mother would not able to afford school fees, having instead to rely on charity or the workhouse. However the comment shows the eagerness some mothers had in getting their children an education in the Parish.

There were three pay schools and two Sunday Schools in the townlands nearest Rossnaglliagh; in Prehen, Ballyore and Gortin.

Prehen School, held in a hamlet called the Barracks, was established in 1818 and by 1824 the master was Robert Dinsmore, a Covenanter, (later termed a Presbyterian), whose income included £10 from pupils, a house and 20 acres of land from Colonel Knox, the patron. The school house was built by Knox at a cost of £50 and two acres of the land were rent free. Attending the school were 12 Church of Ireland, 19 Presbyterian and 25 Roman Catholic pupils. Books were supplied by the Kildare Place Society.

Robert Dinsmore continued to teach at Prehen School in 1834 and the number of pupils by the Protestant return was 9 Church of Ireland, 38 Presbyterian and 45 Roman Catholic. He was to earn £18 annually but this was later amended to £12 - £8 from London Hibernian Society and £4 from the pupils. The Society provided the spelling books, and the Old and New Testament was part of the curriculum.

Occasional visitors included Reverends Carey and Maughan. Ninety six pupils were registered and of these 8 were Church of Ireland, 40 Presbyterian and 48 Roman Catholic. [6]

A Sunday school in Prehen was also under Robert Dinsmore with two other teachers who taught 28 pupils.

In 1824 a school was set up in the townland of Ballyon (Ballyore?) with a master called Allen Broderick (aged 50), who also had income from land. This was a pay school with an income of 12 pounds per annum, of which the London Hibernian Society gave 6 pounds a year. The school was made of stone and lime and cost £4 10s. The denominations of the pupils were 15 Church of Ireland, 19 Presbyterian, 19 Roman Catholic and 3 other denominations (not stated) -36 boys and 20 females.

A thatched school house costing £8 was also established in the neighbouring townland of Gortin, on 1st May 1829. A Mr Moore of County Antrim, who owned the estate at Gortin, was the patron of this private school. He paid 6 pounds and the 49 pupils paid a total of £9 pounds towards income. In 1834, this was adjusted to 12 pounds per annum paid by 34 children, 20 Presbyterian, 4 Roman Catholic and 10 other denomination. The pupils brought their own books. A catechism was taught regularly, but no clergy visited. Thomas Macklin, a Covenanter, taught in the school and continued to be the master in 1834.

A Sunday school was also established in Gortin in 1833 with a total of 40 children, visited by Reverends Maughan and Carson. [7]

However, there were about 700 children in the Rossnagalliagh area in 1830's (this includes only the townlands of Ballyore, Clampernow, Craigtown, Drumagore, Gortin, Gortinure, Tully Upper and Lower, Tirkeeveney, Kittybane, and Tagherina) which would include those not of school age. If half this number were of school age it would seem that about only one fifth of the children between 5 and 15 would have been able to afford to attend the schools in the area, thus falling lower than the whole Parish level of one quarter.

For over 30 years commissioners and enquiries had discussed the inadequateness of pay or hedge schools, such as those discussed above. They were provided and supported in many cases by religious groups which caused controversy over religion and commissioners felt "sowed the seeds of denominationalism". It had also been evident that they did not meet the needs of a rapidly growing population.

1   Ordnance Survey Memoirs , p91

2   Lyons, F S L, Ireland since the Famine, London 1989, p 83 –In 1898 G Balfour found Irish education statistics to be unreliable as they could be based on either Protestant or Catholic returns-see G Balfour -The Educational System of GB and Ireland , London 1898

3   Colby, Col., Ordnance Survey of the County of Londonderry, 1990, p155

4   Londonderry Standard, May 1839

5   Ordnance Survey Memoirs , p 9

6   Ibid   p91, 95

7   Ibid   p87

CHAPTER 2

A SCHOOL AT ROSSNAGALLIAGH

The first mention of a school in Rossnagalliagh was of a "Sunday" school being established in 1835 with 14 male and 12 female pupils. The number of pupils was later adjusted to 24, and included a superintendant, John Ward, and two teachers. These "Sunday" schools could provide both a moral and intellectual education. [1]

The earliest mention of setting up a National school in Rossnagalliagh was recorded by the Honourable the Irish Society (henceforth called the Irish Society) Deputation who visited the area on 10th October 1835. This may have been in response to "a memorial presented to the Irish Society by the inhabitants of the neighbourhood who are very anxious to have a school built for the education of their children". [2]

This appeal for a National school in the area seems to have been made at the same date as the "Sunday" school was established and may have followed the pattern found elsewhere as the National Board took over schools already in place.

The Ordnance Survey memoirs reported a sum of £50 being lately (around 1835) granted by the Irish Society towards the erection of a National school in Rossnagalliagh, with a marginal note that it should be for practical instruction. A further £50 was to be paid when the building was roofed. [3]

The Irish Society archives in 1879 affirmed, "This school which is on the Society's estate, and to which a grant of £15 is annually made, was erected in 1839 and affords primary education to the several religious denominations in the neighbourhood". [4]

The school is recorded to have been taken into connection with the National Board on 7th February 1839. It was to be a non-vested school, which meant it was not vested in the Board, but in local trustees. [5]

Although inspector's reports, school rolls and report books, as well as Irish Society records show the date of the school opening to be 1839, a grant form asking for aid to build a school in Rossnagalliagh is dated 9th November 1843, sent to the Board on 13th November, and received by them on 17th November. The applicants also mentioned the promise by the Irish Society of £50, made in the 1830's, when the school building was roofed in.

Was the grant asked for in retrospect as the form had also included a "maybe" date of 24th January 1839?

The form was sent by a Mr. Thomas White from the Waterside, on behalf of local representatives, and showed the cost of the school to be £166 11s 8d. This appears to be one of the most expensive schools in the district which, according to the applicants, was to facilitate 90 male and 60 female pupils, the highest intake of pupils in any of the surrounding townlands of the Parish. In comparison a National School which was to accommodate 93 pupils at Ballyshaskey cost £65 in1834. [6]

In response to the form, the Board could have paid part of the cost in 1843, as by 1845 the National Board agreed to pay two thirds of the cost towards the expense of setting up new schools alongside local communities or individuals who paid one third, but they had to be vested in the Board, not in trustees as in Rossnagalliagh. (Five years later 3,000 schools were still non-invested and 1,500 vested and by 1900, 5,000 were non-invested and 3,400 vested.)

However, it may be that the Irish Society had paid the total cost, as along with the £100 in 1835 and when the school was roofed in, they made a further contribution of £80.10s towards the building cost in 1845, two years after the form was sent to Dublin.

The Education Commissioners published a series of standardised architectural plans for use by local groups receiving grant aid for school buildings, depending on the intake of pupils. Most were plain, unadorned, single- storey buildings, generally resembling domestic architecture. Some may also have incorporated the Victorian belief in segregating the sexes, which meant separate entrances for boys and girls, or completely separate classrooms or schools.

The dimensions of the school were 60 ft long 20 ft wide and 9 ft high and the applicants put the size of the two schoolrooms at 20ft by 16 ft, but a note written in pencil, probably by the Board, states the rooms were 31 ft by 10 ft and 20 ft by 10 ft. There was no master's house or apartments shown in the building as it was not until 1872 that an Act was passed to provide teachers with residences [7]

The finished school, therefore, was to be of considerable size as in Griffith's Valuation of 1858 it is recorded with a rateable value of £4, the same rateable valuation as the local flax mill, while most houses in the area were valued between ten shillings and one pound. [8]

The Valuation states the land where the school was erected was leased from representatives of William C. Babington. However the application showed the ground for the school had been obtained at a nominal rent from Patrick Browne for 31 years and 2 lives, and stated that 10 years had expired. Mr Brown, therefore, may have leased the ground from Babington and sub-let it to those wishing to build the school in 1833. The 1858 rent roll seem to support this as it gave the lessee as heirs of A. C. Babington with 14 sub-tenancies including the school. Irish Society archives show that Babington's lease did not run out until 1877.[9]

The applicants explained that the other schools in the neighbourhood were Glendermott National School, built in 1829, and under the National Board in 1832, Prehen School under Colonel Knox, a school under a rector four miles away, a meeting house school 4 ½ miles away at Rossdowney and one at Selim five miles away. They stated they were all on the Kildare Place system. The school at Ballyorr was no longer there but the Gortin School remained, although it is not mentioned by the applicants.

If the application was successful those applying agreed that one day a week was to be set apart for religious instruction, but only with parents consent. It was envisaged that Protestants and Catholics would be educated together during the week and, to remove discord, religion was to be taught on a Saturday.

The application form also stated that clergy of different denominations had to have access to the school, and parishioners of both denominations needed to agree to the setting up of the school. Those applying had asked for their co-operation. They had also contacted J Robertson, the local School Inspector.

Five days and five hours were to be allowed for literary and moral education along with reading, writing, arithmetic, grammar, geography and history. Only books sanctioned by the Board were to be used, and any teacher not sanctioned by the Board was to be dismissed.

The Board's form also instructed those applying that they expected the inscription "National School" was to be put up "conspicuously" and if the Commissioners (of the National Board) objected to a particular use of the school they (ie the trustees) had to "give it up". The form also indicated that a register was to be kept.

Those who signed the form may have been the same people who had approached the Irish Society in October 1835.

The form is signed by Rev A J McCarron CC and Mr White, a corn merchant from the Waterside, and owner of a salt works in Rossnagalliagh, who were vested as trustees, along with 10 Protestant laymen:-

Thomas Brown of Rossnagalliagh Robert Wilson, Joseph Killbreth?maybe Galbraith, William Adams from Ballyorr, Alex Moorhead, John Dealey? maybe Daly, from Ballyorr, John Godfrey from Primity, Samuel Torry of Rossnagalliagh, James Orr maybe from Ballyorr and George Henry.

Twelve Roman Catholic laymen also signed which included the superintendant of the Sunday School, John Ward from Rossnagalliagh, John W Neag?, Pat Brown of Rossnagalliagh, Edward Phillips, John Sweeny from Rossnagalliagh, George Bratton from Rossnagalliagh, William Cullen from Rossnagalliagh, Michael Brown, George Doherty, Alexander Smyth from Primity, Phillip Dougherty and James Duffy from Primity. [10]

Teacher and income

Along with the application form to the National Board discussed above, the trustees were also applying for aid toward a teacher's salary, also in November 1843. Not all teachers, however, wished to be openly associated with the Government based Board, as G Downes, who helped compile the Ordnance Survey of the Parish in 1837 stated, "there was a reluctance by some of the schoolmasters (who) have a strong desire for assistance from the National Board of Education, although they do not openly express it". [11]

The teacher was called Margaret McNamee and she was aged 25. As the application is written by Mr White, who had vouched for her as he had known her "a number of years", we can therefore assume this was the teacher's proper name rather than the name given in the Irish Society's report in 1844,"Margaret Nauree". [12]

In the application form she was said to have been appointed on 29th December 1842 and started work on 1st January 1843, which was nearly a year before the application was made. There is a note to say that "no salary (is) yet awarded." and to point out that there were no local funds towards her salary.

However, Mr White also writes that the 40 females and 17 males on the rolls paid about £5 annually towards salary and that in the last six months there had been an average of 39 pupils and 34 present daily. The amount paid by each child was around the average for pay schools in the parish. This seems to be more evidence that the school was already set up at Rossnagalliagh, and a probability Margaret McNamee was already teaching there.

Although Mr White claims there were no "local funds" for the teacher's salary, along with the better off pupils who had been paying £5 annually, was probably a payment from the Catholic Church. We do not know if the trustees were successful in their application on behalf of Margaret McNamee, although the National Board were empowered to make grants to **existing schools** for the payment of teachers by 1845.

Nevertheless, in 1844, Margaret McNamee was applying to the Irish Society for "some annual assistance towards enabling her to continue the instruction of the children in this school, the parents of whom are so poor that they cannot allow her even the most moderate remuneration for her services".

The Irish Society looked at her situation and found it as she had stated and that "her exertions were most praiseworthy and had been attended with considerable success". She was granted £2 10s per annum to be paid half yearly, rising to £5 in 1846.[13]

Generally, teacher's incomes were to vary greatly in 19th century Ireland and were, in some cases, as low as labourer's wages (the wages of a labourer in 1837 was about £18 annually). The yearly salaries among the teaching staff in Londonderry (Parish of Templemore) in 1837, however, may give us an idea of the teacher's salaries in the area.

In Ballougry National School, which was built by the Irish Society in 1827 and was a mixed school, the Society granted the school mistress £10 in 1832. However by 1837 the Irish Society paid £30 and the pupils £20 out of which the master, Andrew Gilmour, received £40, and the rest was spent on stationary and repairs. There were 32 pupils. The Irish Society also supported Shantallow School where the master received £32. 2s 0d, London Ladies Society School (Fountain area) the mistress earned £23 and Presbyterian School where the master earned £30 and Mistress £16. In Ballymagrorty School the master received £10.

In St Columb's National School (established in 1825) the teachers' salary was paid by National Board £30; Irish Society £10; Chapel £25 and pupils £9-there were 339 children at the school. The master, Patrick O'Connor, received £30 as did his wife, Susanna. The equality of pay for the mistress is interesting compared to the Presbyterian School. However the large number of children this couple had to teach seems incredible, even if all the children did not attend regularly.[14]

Teacher training

Colonel Colby outlined his assessment of teacher training in the 1830's when he commented, "The teachers are probably as competent as can be expected in a country where general attention has never yet been given to the science of teaching, notwithstanding its prominent, and now acknowledged, importance". [15]

Miss McNamee was not to be a trained teacher, nor had she taught at a national school. This meant she had not been educated at a Kildare Place Model school in Dublin. The Kildare Place Society had been a pioneer in the field from 1811 establishing model schools with residential accommodation for candidate teachers. Although the new National Board had adopted the Kildare Place Society's model schools for teacher training, which was to be inter-denominational in character, it was opposed by the churches.

As a result by 1883 only 27% of Catholic and 52% of Protestant teachers had any formal training when the Board was to bow to church pressure for separate training colleges, and by the turn of the century only half of all teachers were trained. [16]

Mr White had, however, no qualms about Margaret's ability as he wrote on the application form that she was "perfectly competent". Despite the Board having some control over the curriculum, managers (usually clergy) had considerable power in relation to employment of teachers and management of the school.

1   Ordnance survey p 92,93

2   Report presented to Irish Society 10th Oct 1835, p36

3   Ibid

4   Hon Irish Society Archives, Kew – CLA/049/EM/01/051

5   PRONI- ED/6/3/5/1Folio 17- this also includes all the inspectors reports from 1909-1935 covering setting up cookery classes, need for desks, inadequate classroom space, retirement of Mrs Elliot, lighting of school fires, provision of a map, conversion of teachers accommodation and injury of a child.

6   Ordnance Survey, p91, ED1/25/46-85 No 63

7   History of Irish Education, p200

8   In the Shadow, p102

9   V Aldous report to Irish Society, 2002

10   PRONI Mic 5A/9A, 1831 census shows addresses of trustees

11   Ordnance Survey, p26

12   CLA/EM/01/27

13   CLA/049/EM/01/27

14   Colby, p145, 156

15   Ibid, p155

16   Lyons, P86

CHAPTER 3

ROSSNAGALLIAGH'S FIRST PUPILS

The total number of children in the townland of Rossnagalliagh in the period 1831-38 was 71. It was to be the largest populated townland in the area in November 1835 with 33 families recorded in the Ordnance Survey Memoirs, while Ballyore had 30 families, Primity had 26 families and Kittybane had 20 families. Among these families were the first pupils at the school and a substantial proportion were so poor that the teacher had to appeal to the Irish Society for help with her salary in 1844.

Rossnagalliagh's tenants had been living in a very poor state when the Irish Society agent visited land leased by the Babington family as early as 1826 and found "28 mud cabins inhabited by persons of low description". The Irish Society's architect, William Tite, visiting Rossnagalliagh in 1834, suggested the Society should repossess the farm from the Babington family so "that it might become an ornament rather than .....a disgrace to the neighbourhood of Londonderry". [1]

However a report by the Irish Society in October 10th 1835 stated there had been no improvement since the last visit, and in November, 1836 the deputation found "the habitations by the side of the road are of the most wretched description and the ground immediately in front of the hovels is disgustingly filthy ".

As a result the Society once again requested some arrangement whereby the lease would be surrendered into the Society's hands in order that improvements would be made to the property. However, a Miss Babington was still the leaseholder according to Griffiths Valuation in 1858 and as discussed above the family still held the land in 1877.[2]

A number of families at Rossnagalliagh may, therefore, have lived at subsistence level with fathers relying on part-time work as labourers, without being able to benefit from a tied cottage, as this kind of housing had declined by 40% by 1841. (After the Labourer's Act of 1883 and 1885 15,000 cottages with half an acre of land were built, and another 20,000 authorised in Ireland as a whole.) [3]

In 1838 at least 37 spinning wheels are found in 25 homes in Rossnagalliagh indicating the need for additional income from hand spinning. The reliance on an extra income, however, was not confined to Rossnagalliagh as in Lower Tully 30 wheels were in 21 homes, and 30 spinning wheels were in 26 homes in Primity. [4]

Nevertheless, the whole domestic linen industry and particularly the cottage industry, was in a state of collapse due to the introduction of cotton cloth in Britain. Hand spinners were also losing their work locally as they were taken over by larger and more efficient linen firms such as Herdmans in Sion Mills. Added to this hardship, rents were rising alarmingly.

In 1841 the population in Ulster had risen to 2.4 million and about half of these were cottiers, labourers or impoverished spinners and weavers struggling to survive. In the whole parish of Clondermott there were 540 paupers and as many as 480 families of cottiers, some of whom became paupers, and had to beg before harvest time brought relief.Their daily diet included stirabout, oatcakes, buttermilk or potatoes while they were available, but many were not strangers to famine even before and after the Great Famine of 1845.

The children from these backgrounds, therefore, not only were unable to contribute to the teacher's salary, but lacked proper clothing or footwear to walk a distance to school, especially in winter time.

A substantial percentage of the first pupils may have also come from Newbuildings village which was a single street with 37 houses in 1834, and had a population of 150. The houses were reported to have been badly thatched and in poor appearance overall. Most of the houses were low and stone built, only a few had more than one storey.

Some fathers from the village may have had part- time work in a grain mill at Primity or at lime, road or building quarries at Prehen, but most were occasional labourers relying heavily on spinning. [5]

Background to pupils- 1860 to 1900
Between 1860 and the beginning of the 20th century, pupils' addresses took in many townlands in the surrounding district. They were to be the most widespread at any time in the school's history.

They included -The Bolies, Kittybane, Greerstown, Primity, Rossnagalliagh, Lower and Upper Tully, Clampernow, Magheramason, Gortin, Ballyorr, Dunhugh (Dunhue), Coolmaghery, Prehen, Magheracannon, Brick kilns, Craigtown, Creaghcor, Gortinure, Drumagor, Keery, Gortmonley, Tagherina, Glenderowen, Londonderry, Cloghogle, Tamneymore, Bogagh, Drumcorkin and Castlemellon.

Examples of fathers' occupations from the school register give us an insight into the wide variety of trades which were found in the area, and an indication of some of the better off pupils who attended Rossnagalliagh.

Shopkeepers or shopkeeper/publicans in Newbuildings - Henry,McDevitt, McKeever, McLaughlin, Kerr

Scutchers- Boyle from Greerstown, McCloskey and Devine from Newbuildings

Shoemakers- McDermott from Primity, Lynch from Ballyorr

Blacksmiths- Thompson from Coolmaghery, Tedley from Primity, McCurry and Strawbridge from Newbuildings

Mason- Orr from Primity

Carpenter-Walker from Primity, Coulter from Keery, McCafferty from Dunhue

Tailor –McVerit from Prehen

Chemist- McLaughlin from Magheramason

Coachman-McCloskey from Gortin

Insurance agent- Colhouns from Magheramason

Merchant- McCarter from Lower Tully

Railway Engineer-Burke from Newbuildings

The majority of pupils in the latter decades of the 19th century, however, continued to come from farming or labouring backgrounds, and as the demand for shirts increased in local factories, many mothers worked as "outworkers". Farmer or labourer's wives may also have supplemented the family income with the sale of eggs.

Health and attendance

The health of children generally was causing alarm at this time, but those taking an interest in the subject believed it may, in part, be due to conditions at school.

"Lancet" wrote to the Londonderry Journal in 21st April 1880 that the medical profession should therefore,

"Struggle for a better hygienic condition of schools and school houses than at present prevails...in respect to the ventilation of school rooms, the length of time spent in study, the method of studying, the posture of the body and management of light with consequent strain on eyesight of children" [6]

We have no exact description of the school rooms at Rossnagalliagh when it first opened although most were similar in style.

Typical schoolroom showing long desks with inkwells and forms, teacher's desk and blackboards

Like many other national schools, the schoolroom was heated by an open fire. In most areas the pupils would have helped with the heating costs by bringing turf for the fire, but as early as 1832 there was a scarcity of fuel in the Newbuildings area as turf bogs were exhausted, and timber was also scarce as the population rose. The nearest source of turf, therefore, was Lisdillion, Lower Cumber or Donagheady,which would have meant travelling between four to seven miles, and being able to afford 12 pounds for an acre of bog. In 1848 6 loads of turf cost 10d a load and in 1849 half a ton cost about 7 shillings. [7]

It was not until 1911 that the Government provided funds for heating in schools.

Ill health, lack of proper clothing or footwear and the need to bring an income into the home, in addition to the poor conditions in some schoolrooms, was to ensure low attendance as the century ended.

Attendance by pupils, however, was to be voluntary in the new national schools. The subject was to be raised at a Teacher's Association in the Strabane area of Co. Tyrone in 1880 when they insisted that there was "a need for the introduction of compulsory attendance of not less than 150 days annually ....(which) would be productive of excellent results both in education and disciplinary point of view".

By 1898 a local Government Act brought in compulsory attendance, mostly aimed at urban schools. Each rural and urban area had School Attendance Committees which were set up to ensure pupils, aged 6 to 14, attended the state -aided schools for at least 150 days a year. This helped attendances to grow so that by 1890's 60% of pupils attended school, rising to 75% in 1908. [8]

Religious background of Pupils
According to the sources available the following pupils attended between1860-1900:-

1860's - 31 Roman Catholic, 32 Presbyterian and 10 Irish
or Established Church (by 1st March 1869 termed Church of Ireland)
1870's - 62 Roman Catholic, 105 Presbyterian, and 15 Church of Ireland
1880's - 53 Roman Catholic, 98 Presbyterian and 18 Church of Ireland
1890's - 71 Roman Catholic, 62 Presbyterian, 18 Church of Ireland
and 2 Methodist
1900-10- 83 Roman Catholic, 72 Presbyterian, 17 Church of Ireland
and 5 Methodist

Roman Catholic and Presbyterian pupils were to remain the majority of pupils at Rossnagalliagh. The number of Church of Ireland pupils were always to be smaller, although there were 114 Established Church families in the area in 1839.

Only two Methodist families, called Clements and Orr, are found in the roll books available. In the 1830's the number of Methodists in the Parish was too small "for the creation of a fund to raise houses of worship" and as a result they met in the open air for services.

However, there must have been quite a few Methodist families in the Newbuildings area by 1853 as a new church was built at this time. The Methodist children would have attended a day school in the church grounds but it was closed by the end of the 19th century. These children may then have gone to school in Londonderry. [9]

1   Report to Irish Society 1826, 1834, 1835 Curl, p246, p248

2   Report to Irish Society November 26th 1836, Curl p256

3   Lyons, p51

4   Ordnance Survey, p133

5   In the Shadow of the Tail of the Fox, pages 45-66

6   Londonderry Journal 21st April, 1880

7   Ordnance Survey, p15,25

8   Lyons, p88

9   Reed, Charles, An Historical Narrative of the Origins and Constitution of the Honourable the Irish Society- Appendix lists colleges schools and other institutions receiving annual grants –p55 includes Rossnagalliagh Wesleyan Methodist School and Rossnagalliagh Wesleyan Methodist Sabbath School- although the church and school was to be built in Primity – it also lists a grant to the teacher of Rossnagalliagh School p54. By 1853 the teacher , church and new Methodist school were getting grants from the Irish Society – also see A short history of Methodism in Londonderry by Earnest Gordon Laird

CHAPTER 4

THE CURRICULUM AND CHANGES
1860-1900

In addition to the pupils attending school between the ages of 6-14, were those taking approved courses and undergoing examinations. They could be taught until they were 18 years old, although some at Rossnagalliagh were still taking classes in their 20's. These classes would have been taken after school hours. Margaret McNamee taught these older students extra curriculum subjects such as music and drawing, but also the three R's. This augmented her salary as she was paid by the results of the examinations.

Extra classes in subjects such as arithmetic, cost five shillings a pupil, and were to be delivered one hour twice a week, therefore not all parents could afford them. Nevertheless it is interesting to look at the examples below, particularly noting the considerable fees paid by Mary McLaughlin, who was an orphan, or Maggie Doherty, the child of a labourer.

Sample of the fees paid in 1876/77:-
Ellen McMurray - father a mechanic- fees 2s
Jane Devine-father a shoemaker, fees 12s 8d
Maggie Doherty -father a labourer-fees 17s 3d
Isabella Stuart-father a farmer-fees 51s 10d
Mary McLaughlin – orphan fees 21s 2d

For examinations to take place an examination roll was prepared showing the names of all the pupils who had made 100 or more attendances during the previous year, preceding the month of examinations. The examinations were then carried out by inspectors who recorded the results. In early 1870 an x indicated a pass and o a failure but later in the decade "1" denoted a satisfactory pass and "2" a mere pass.

William Brown, who started Rossnagalliagh in 1865 at the age of 11, was to sit the following examinations in 1872. In the second and third class he undertook reading, spellings, writing and arithmetic examinations, all of which he passed. However, in 1873, he was to pass only writing and arithmetic. He also attempted a music examination but failed. He was struck off the register in 1874. He was 20 years old.

Bessie Crawford aged 11, who had not attended a national school before coming to Rossnagalliagh on 11th September 1865, was to be examined on reading, spelling, writing, arithmetic grammar, geography, needlework, music and drawing. Her fees were 12 shillings a year. Her father was a farmer.

Eliza Crawford (she may have been Bessie's sister) was not to have attended national school before coming to Rossnagalliagh at the age of 9, on 20th September 1866. She was to do similar examinations as Bessie. Her father paid the following fees- 16 shillings on 31st May 1876, 11 shillings 31st May 1877 and 10 shillings 1 penny on 31st May 1878. It would seem she was still attending classes when she was in her 20's.

Jane McClure came from Killymallaght to live at Tagherina and attended Rossnagalliagh from 31st July 1873. Jane's family paid 7 shillings on 31st May 1877; 8 shillings and 4 pence on 31st May 1878; 9 shillings on 31st May 1879; 8 shillings and 2 pence on 31st May 1880; 3 shillings and 6 pence on 30th April 1881. Her father was a farmer.

Matilda Orr from Ballyorr had not been to a national school before coming to Rossnagalliagh on 18th February 1867. She was to sit examinations on 31st October 1872 and 31st August 1873. We have no record of any fees but are told she passed all her examinations.

Margaret McCloskey from Newbuildings came to Rossnagalliagh on 29th January 1867. She had never attended national school before. Margaret was to sit the same examinations as the Crawford girls in her third and fourth year, but did not do music or drawing. Her father was a scutcher and did not pay any fees for her.

It is unclear if any prizes were awarded to pupils generally for excellence in examinations in the second half of the nineteenth century. A merit certificate award could be given, however, to every pupil 13 years old and over who had been in 7th Grade and inspectors' felt had reached a good proficiency in English, arithmetic and geography.

An Intermediate Education Act of 1878 had introduced indirect funding under which grants were made to schools on the basis of the performance of pupils in these examinations. A meeting of Strabane Teachers Association in May 1880, however, was to discuss the "payment by results" system as it was not proving popular.

The Association argued "that they (teachers)should be relieved from all contingency of payment as depending on passes in particular subjects, or in collection of fees, in many cases too stringent for those capable of studying such subjects".They called instead for better pay in keeping with English and Scotch teachers.

The Association must have been representative of the feelings of teachers nationwide as the system of "payments by results" was dropped in 1900. The Commissioners compensated teachers by making a corresponding increase in their salaries, as they had in 1892 when fees were abolished.

In addition to the subjects described above, senior girls in Grades 4-7 had domestic economy. Classes were being held as early as 1872 as shown in Rebecca Thompson's domestic economy book. The book outlined the purpose of the course as it stated that "this science which belongs specially to the education ofgirls is more important in the household than all the other arts and sciences together."

It claimed that the influence and power of girls, therefore, was enormous. They had to do with "success or failure, with happiness or misery, quite as much as statesmen or philanthropists, though, in different ways." Although the book acknowledged the girls had a "high mission" and that there was talk of women having rights, they were not to be deprived of "the holy and blessed right of making happy homes".

Depending on the family's economic status girls no longer married at 16, nor those of 20 or above considered old maids as in 1830's, but the marriageable age had not yet reached that found in 1911, when the average age of marriage for women was 28.[1]

It is unclear if the girls of Rossnagalliagh School were aware of their high calling or responsibilities, but the book clearly shows their allotted role in society.

On a lighter note the book instructed the girls not to follow fashion as it would affect their health by making "artificial waists with stays, or load their head with weight in the shape of pads and false hair, to wear tight collars, or to wear tight shoes or high heels".

School books and equipment
Although National Education was free, books had to be paid for. The National Board provided cheap text books for reading, spelling, writing, arithmetic and a little geography, although in some cases, where necessary, the poorer children did not have to pay for books. School text books, therefore, were to be continually in use, and handed down from older to younger members of the family, and even parent to child. This practice was to continue into the 20th century.

The cost of school books and equipment in 1890 was as follows:-
First book of Arithmetic, one and half pence each; English Grammar, 2 pence each; Outlines of Geography, 3d pence each; Introduction to Geography, 4 pence each; Table Books, half -penny each; Vere Foster Copy Books – varied grades, 1 penny each; Exercise Books, one penny each; Note Books, one penny each.

Despite many school teachers being poorly paid, the Powis Report of 1868 had showed many teachers provided essentials for the classroom such as steel nibs which cost 6 pence per gross; a quart of black ink at 6 pence, slate pencils at 2 pence per 100 or 100 holders at 6 pence. Teachers also provided any maps or charts. [2]

Punishment at School
Corporal punishment was an accepted part of national school life and was not to be abolished in some areas until 1986. For example there are accounts of children being punished for writing with their left hand in 1950's.

Each National School had to keep a Corporal Punishment Book in which the teacher recorded the date, name of the pupil, standard, offence, nature and amount of punishment, and his/her own signature.

Only the Principal could inflict punishment, and he/she had to allow ten minutes to elapse between the offence and the punishment, and to enter the particulars in the book **before** punishing the child. The teachers were instructed by the Board that

"The boxing of ears and pulling their hair and similar ill-treatment was absolutely forbidden and will be visited with severe penalties".

Teachers in some schools punished the children with a ferule or rattan (bamboo) cane. Corporal Punishment Books indicate that the punishment was to have been two light slaps.

Offences, taken from another national school book, which give a glimpse into what was thought to deserve punishment at the end of the nineteenth century, included-
Mitching and then speaking back impudently.
Continuing to work sums with ink and pen carelessly, having been reasoned with and threatened.
Disobedience and rubbing out lines with fingers.
Stealing the gooseberries and making themselves sick.
Refusing to speak in an audible voice.
Not attending to his teacher and putting a large spittle on his hands.

Refusing to sing. Singing at school was not purely for pleasure as it had many rules which may have not been appreciated by some pupils. While singing they had to "stand with their heels together" and if sitting it should be upright "to make free play of muscles required for breathing". School bags were not allowed on backs while singing, heads were to be "erect, not thrown back, shoulders back, not up, mouths freely open, arms by the side, not folded, breathing through the nose not the mouth." [3]

Leaving the playground at playtime.[4] This last offence seems to have been an ongoing problem at Rosssnagalliagh. Paddy Brown, a pupil from 1905 to 1914, claimed pupils played on the main Strabane to Londonderry road, which was in front of the school. However it would have been mostly traffic free and therefore have been of little risk. Few had motor cars, travelling instead by jaunting car, pony and trap or farm cart, and most goods were sent by train.

A Change of Staff and Additions to the School
The age of retirement for teachers was to be part of a discussion by the Strabane Teachers' Association meeting in May 1880. They called for a reduction from 60 years for females and 65 for males with a full pension, to 60 for males and 55 for

females. However the discussion was not to affect Margaret McNamee as she had retired by 1877, when she was around 60 years old. She was succeeded by Mary Jane Curry, who was appointed Principal on 1st January 1877, and by 1884, the staff also included a monitor, Jane Hanna.

Although quite a high number of monitors, such as Jane, were teaching in National schools, a meeting of the National Board and Raphoe Catholic clergy on June 18th1880, reported that the managers were disappointed at the number of monitors and teachers who failed to get promotion at the Easter examination. They believed that not only was the examination set at too high a standard but also that the employment of assistants, work mistresses and monitors in national schools "is excessively high and injurious to education." [5]

The Principal was also to apply to the Board in Dublin for aid towards the salary of an assistant, Sarah Crumley, who was 20 years old. Sarah began to teach on 1st July, 1884, although, like many other assistants at that time she had not had any formal teacher training. This was Sarah's first teaching post for which she received £27 annually. [6]

Changes in the School Building

By 1879 the school classroom was proving to be too small. Although it was supposed to accommodate 150, and only 70 are recorded as attending when District Inspector William Rob(?)had made a visit that year, Mary Jane Curry may have moved into the school after the 1872 Act was passed allowing teachers to have accommodation. Mary Jane, therefore, approached the Irish Society for help and "memoralised for an enlargement of the school premises, the schoolroom being found incapable of affecting accommodation to the project in attendance".

Applying for a grant from the National Board may not have been an option at this time as it was being investigated by the Crown Treasury about the amount spent on buildings and improvement grants. Consequently the Treasury moved "to curb the spendthrift tendencies of the National Education Commission".

The Irish Society's General Agent reported favourably on the application and recommended "it be referred to the surveyor to prepare plans and estimates for such suitable enlargement of the premises as will meet the requirements of the school." [7]

A year later, in 1880, the Society's agent report seems to have re-thought enlarging the original school as they reported, "The plans of the proposed new school at Rossnagalliagh were laid before us without any specification. The surveyor roughly estimates the cost of erection at about £500. We are of the opinion that a suitable building could be obtained for a smaller outlay and recommend further consideration thereof be adjourned at present, and that the surveyor be requested to furnish an alternative plan with specification". [8]

William Harte, surveyor for the Society from 1874, was asked to design the new school. Plans show a schoolhouse and teachers residence in an Italiate Rundbogenstil manner. [9]

However the Society did not carry out the plans for a new school as Mary Jane Curry paid £40 towards an extension herself, which was reimbursed by the Society.

1   Connolly, Sean, Patterns of Marriage, in Familia Vol 2 No 8 , 1992, p87

2   Turner, John, Magheramason, 1878-1978, P31- capital punishment information also from Turner, 1878-1978

3   Notes for teachers-Instructions for National Schools, p27

4   Turner, p86

5   Londonderry Journal, May 1880, Londonderry Journal, June 1880

6   PRONI–EDI/27/290-317/45

7   Irish Society Archives, Kew CLA/049/EM/01/051

8   Ibid CLA/049/EM/01/052

9   Curl, J S The Londonderry Plantation, p284,311

CHAPTER 5

THE SCHOOL IN THE EARLY 20TH CENTURY

Between 1905 and 1914 the Principal, Mrs Elliott (nee Mary Jane Curry), taught with a Mrs Gill and Miss Reynalds and by 1918, had been joined by her daughter, Mary Nugent Elliott. Mrs Elliott was 62 years of age.

Late 19th Century.Mrs Elliot is on the right.

Mrs Elliott is on the right holding a small child. Other teachers may have been Mrs Gill and Miss Reynalds. c1905-1914. Note some children are bare footed but all seem to be well dressed.

The pupils in this period came from Glenderowen, Magheracannon, Coolmaghery, Newbuildings, Donemana Road, Dam Row, Quay Lane, Dunhugh, Gortinure, Clampernow, Rossnagalliagh, Hillhead, Magheramason, Ballyorr, Primity, Gortin, Kittybane, Lower Tully, Warbleshinney, Waterside, Cullion and Gortmonley.

Between1911-22 the religious make up of the children were 97 Roman Catholic, 70 Presbyterian, 14 Church of Ireland and 6 Methodists.

In the first decades of the 20th century the majority of the children continued to come from labouring families.

School Building and Equipment

As the school building had now to accommodate the Principal and her growing family, space continued to be at a premium. The allowance of eight foot per pupil meant the ideal number of children to be accommodated was 64 although Paddy Browne's account at the end of the chapter claimed 130-140 attended between 1905 and 1914, but the numbers cannot be verified as all rolls are not available.

An Inspectors report in 1909 showed the size of the two classrooms - 33ft 4 inches x 16 ft 3 ins x 10ft 6 in high and 26ft 11 ins x 16 ft 4 ins and 10ft 6ins high – around the same as the original dimensions found in the grant form of 1843, but this does not include the extension of 1880.[1]

However Paddy Brown's account tells that there was only one classroom used when he attended from 1905 to 1914. The other classroom therefore, may have been used as living accommodation, and the extension in 1880 may have been the addition of a kitchen and attic rooms.

On 3rd November, 1911, the Inspector who called at the school did not comment on the lack of classroom space, but wrote that "a supply of suitable desks has been provided for the children". Nevertheless, Mrs Elliott wrote to the Board again on 19th October 1915 complaining of the lack of room for the 79 pupils present on that date, and commented there was only room for 56 pupils.

Mrs Elliott was of the opinion that the "attendance shall be limited to what there is room for by removal of the younger people." In response Reverend McFeely, who had taken over as manager of the school from Reverend McFaul, stated that he was considering the reduction of numbers in school. However the Inspector's report indicated that no action was to be taken immediately.

By 3rd July 1916 the Manager was reported to have desks made suitable for juniors and would "consider the question of overcrowding". However, in January 1917, Mr Ellis, school Inspector, found there were only 47 children present out of a total of 81, and when he called again on 29th February only 37 out of a total of 78 were present.

The low numbers at this time may have been due, in part, to winter conditions. Nevertheless by 7th December1917 the Inspector recorded that "the overcrowding was not serious" but included the instructions "note and wait."

War conditions seem to be the main reason for not solving the accommodation problem and, as the Inspector's reports show, the matter seems to have been put on hold at this time. [2]

New direction for education
Education for most national school pupils in the first decades of the 20th century was still to be rudimentary and at best, mechanical. Many children remained in school only until they attained functional literacy.

In an attempt to overcome low educational standards new thinking had been announced by The Commission on Manual and Practical Instruction (or Belmore Commission). They had reported in 1898 that Ireland should be brought into line with educational thinking in Europe, which concentrated on practical and child-centred education, and a member of the Board, William Starkie, implemented the recommendations in the revised Programme for National Schools by 1900.

Class teaching, therefore, was to be replaced by "draft teaching". This meant that Standards were grouped, and all in the group needed to share the same lesson. Putting children into groups was thought to lighten the load in one and two teacher schools, and to promote efficient teaching. The curriculum from the 1918-1922 Roll Book indicates that Rossnagalliagh's pupils, in line with the new National Board thinking, were now divided into groups. Note the numbers in brackets below within a grade/standard for different subjects.

Infants (under 5's) at Rossnagalliagh were taught to speak well before they tried to read. Their curriculum included:-

Reading, Occupation (unclear what this means), Writing, Number, Recreation, Drawing (1,2,3,) and Number, Occupation and Oral English (4,5)

Interestingly the Board instructed that slates were not to be used in infant classes on sanitary as well as educational grounds, and that all desk work should be done on paper, which they claimed was now cheap. This idea was not implemented within the Infant class in Rossnagalliagh.

Grade or Standard 1 and 2-
Writing, Arithmetic, Reading, Written Arithmetic, Transcription, Oral English, Recreation, Information (unclear what this means) (1,2,3) Reading (4,5) Composition (1,2,3) Arithmetic (4,5) Handwork(1) Reading (2) Drawing (3,4,5)

Grade or Standard 3 and 4-
English Oral (1,2,3,4) or Written (5), Arithmetic, Reading, Oral English, (1,2) Composition (3,4,5), Needlework (1,2,3,) PT(4,5), Religious Instruction

Grade or Standard 5 and 6-
English-Oral and Written, Arithmetic, Composition, Geography, Silent Reading (1,2), Reading (3,4,5), Recreation, Geography (1), Nature Study (2,4), Hygiene (3), English (5), Singing (1,2), Drawing, Needlework (1,2,3), PT (4,5), Religious Instruction-(prayers, catechism and sacred history) was taught to Roman Catholic pupils in Standards 3-7 at the end of the school day for half an hour, while the Protestant children went home.

Higher Grades or Standards presumably would have followed Grade or Standard 5 and 6 as pages showing these Grades are missing.

Examination subjects undertaken in this period are given in this example of pupil Sara McGrory, from Newbuildings.

Sara began school in 1911 at the age of 6. In infant class she did reading, spellings, writing and arithmetic examinations. In 1913 she was in Grade 2 and undertook reading, spellings, writing, arithmetic and needlework examinations for 1st Grade. In 1914 she was in 3rd Grade but doing 2nd Grade examinations in reading, spelling, writing, arithmetic, needlework, drawing and singing.

In 1915 she remained in 3rd Grade and did that Grades' examinations which included reading, spelling, writing, arithmetic, grammar, geography needlework, drawing and singing. In 1916 she was in 4th Grade and did that Grades' examinations, reading, spellings, writing, arithmetic, grammar, needlework, drawing and singing. In 1917 she did the same examinations as in 1916, but for the 5th Grade and she repeated the same examinations in 1918 again for the 5th Grade. Sara was to leave school on 19th October 1918 aged 13.

Literacy

The Board also recommended that more time should be spent on composition and less on dictation, and that increased attention should be paid to infants, as in the past the tendency was to overlook them in comparison to seniors. They felt this had "injurious consequences as the pupils got bad habits at an early stage which were difficult to eradicate later". Senior pupils were, therefore, still learning to write in 5th, 6th or 7th Grade and still writing "headline copies".

In 1851 47% of children 5 years and over could neither read or write, and in 1871 the figure was 33%. However, by 1911, the percentage of over 5 years of age that remained illiterate had fallen to 12%, while those who could read only fell from 20% to 4%. [3]

The National Board, therefore, encouraged a wider and more interesting range of reading material to replace reading tablets which, they believed, had produced "mechanical teaching and unintelligent reading".The teachers of infants particularly were felt to have had relied on these reading sheets or tablets.

By today's standard some of the Board's reading books would be seen as too difficult for the ages they were intended, and the subject matter of little interest to the boys and girls. Pupils' progression in school, nevertheless, was commonly denoted by"the book he is on".

In theory, the managers of the school would have had an input to this material, but the Board had to examine them and sanction their use. At annual inspections pupils were only examined from the Board's books, and their teachers were tested for their classification by their acquaintance with them.

Reading books used at Rossnagalliagh therefore came under the Educational Series of Story Readers by the Educational Company of Ireland Limited (Dublin and Belfast). Rebecca McCorkell's (pupil 1918) reading book was called "Lost and Found -The Adventures of a Boy Singer" by Madge E Denny.

Her sister, Maggie's reading book (pupil 1916) was produced under The New World School Series, and called "Granny's Wonderful Chair" by Frances Browne. (Browne and Nolan Ltd Dublin, Belfast, Cork and Waterford) Frances was a blind poetess and writer from Stranorlar, Co Donegal.

The contents of the book included:-
The Christmas Cuckoo, The Lords of the White and Grey Castles, The Greedy Shepherd, The Story of the Fairyfoot, The Story of the Childe Charity Sour and Civil, The Story of Merry Mind, Prince Wisewit's Return.

Another text book used at Rossnagalliagh was called "The Treasure House of Literature" – a Junior Book by the Educational Company.

Below is a small sample of the chapters in the book:-
Abraham Lincoln, The retreat from Moscow, The Story of Regulus, A Lesson on Nest Building, The Japanese, The story of the Pyramids, How Rubber is made, The Ostrich, How Cu-Chulainn got his name and Orpheus and Eurydice.

There were also poems and shortened stories by authors such as William Blake, Robert Louis Stevenson, Oliver Goldsmith, George Eliot and John Greenleaf Whittier. At the back of the book were lists of difficult words taken from the book which the pupils may have had as spellings or subjects for sentences.

Practical Courses for the Older Girl
The popularity of women agitating for the vote in the early 20th century and the aims of the suffragette movement did not filter down into the classroom, and as a

result girls were expected to marry, remain in the home and look after the family. Older girls in 5th Grade upwards, therefore, continued to be taught domestic economy which included instruction on how to cook and sew and be thrifty housewives. Darning was thought by the Board to be "very useful and one of the most needed subjects in which girls can be trained ". The Board's manual for teachers in 1913 asked"how is the family foot-gear to be kept in order unless the woman of the family knows how to darn it"? [4]

Although cookery was deemed an "extra " subject before 1900, by 1914 classes for older girls were thought by the Board to be beneficial.Teachers were reminded by the Board that "they have the privilege of helping to form the characters and habits of future wives and mothers of the country". The course included making simple food and being taught how to ensure cleanliness, order, economy and thrift was found in the home. [5]

Left: Small cookery class.
The date is unknown.

On 13th January 1909 an Inspectors' report indicated that there was hope that cookery would "be taken up next year" at Rossnagalliagh and on 5th September 1910 the Board agreed that an assistant would be able to teach cookery in winter if she could get instruction at the Technical School in Londonderry. The photograph overleaf was taken around 1911and shows that a Miss McCann had taken up the post. [6]

Free grants were also supposed to be available from the Board in 1913 to gain necessary "apparatus" for new subjects which were to be included into the syllabus such as Nature Study, Elementary Science or Hygiene. The Board was eager to promote these courses which highlighted food values and weather observations, the dangers of wet clothing and damp housing, domestic and personal cleanliness and eradicating bad habits such as "scratching the head, sucking the pencil or fingers, moistening the fingers to turn a page, coughing, sneezing or yawning without covering the mouth." However war conditions and lack of funds delayed Rossnagalliagh gaining the necessary "apparatus" for these new courses. [7]

Cookery class with Miss McCann c1911 –the girls were expected to cover their hair and wear sleeve attachments and white aprons when cooking.

Temperance Lessons

All Grades from 5-7 had temperance lessons. In the nineteenth century there had been a temperance society in the village of Newbuildings to promote sobriety which may have been in response to the fact that there were four spirit dealers in such a small village. According to those undertaking the Ordnance Survey in the area in 1837, however, it had been "due to the want of money and decline in profit of cottage spinning, due to mills". [8]

It is interesting to note the reasons given to pupils in the early 20th century for not drinking alcohol or starting too young to smoke. Unlike today's thinking which links drinking or smoking with serious disease, those on the Education Board seemed to concentrate on moral and economic reasons, which reflected the concerns of the day.

The school children were taught that alcohol was a stimulant and "acts like a whip to a tired horse; it enables a person to use up his food more quickly but leaves him more exhausted afterwards". Alcohol affected the brain and injured the digestion but its moral and social degradation was "so obvious that no further argument is needed against its use". It was also seen as a habit that led to "great waste of time and inattention to duty, and is a very expensive luxury".

The children were also to learn of the dangers of smoking in youth as they had not stopped growing, and like alcohol, was a very expensive habit and "may lead to waste of time and to the drinking habit". However, it was not to be fully condemned by those on the National Board who ended the advisory notes by stating "to some it (smoking) acts as a poison, to others completely harmless". [9]

Cigarettes were widely used in the early years of the century and many young men took up the habit of chewing tobacco. Cigarettes were also part of a soldier's rations during the First World War.

Impact of World War 1
Although some men in the Newbuildings area had initially enrolled in the Irish Volunteers, there is evidence that fathers of pupils and past pupils had taken the King's shilling and joined up.

George McLaughlin (pupil 1945-52) recalled that John Kerr from Ballyorr (a pupil in 1900) had been in a cavalry regiment. Patrick O'Donnell (a pupil in 1907) from Newbuildings, had joined the RAF, but died from influenza on 28th October 1918, and was buried at Ardmore. John Campbell (pupil 1898) and Andrew Campbell (pupil 1900) both joined the 12th Royal Inniskillen Fusilers.

There was no disruption to school life due to the war apart from not dealing with the overcrowding problem and ensuring the necessary equipment was available for new courses. The closely packed classroom, however, may have acted as an incubator for an epidemic of scarletina which eventually closed the school for the month of September until 22nd October 1917. Maybe as a response to outbreaks such as this the Board offered advice on how to keep schools clean and how lavatories or outhouses should be kept, with floors washed and dusted regularly.

After the war ended in November 1918 the children at Rossnagalliagh got a holiday for the whole month of December. It may have been at the instigation of the Rev. McFeely, manager of the school, who was also chaplain to the Catholic forces at Ebrington Barracks. He had previously performed an unveiling ceremony of a grotto erected by the Royal Inniskillen Fusiliers at St Columb's Church, Waterside. A brass plate acknowledging the event was placed in the church. There may have been fathers of pupils and past pupils involved in the ceremony. [10]

1   ED/6/3/5/1 Folio 17

2   ED 6/3/5/1

3   Lyons, p88

4   Instructions for National
     Schools P 73/74

5   Instructions for National Schools P112

6   ED 6/3/1 Folio 17

7   ED 6/3/5/1

8   Ordnance survey, p15

9   Instructions for national Schools p 100

10   Derry Journal May 29th 1916

Personal recollections

Paddy Brown attended Rossnagalliagh from 1905-14. Carmel Gallagher, a pupil at the school in the 1970's, interviewed Paddy as part of a project.

Paddy lived at Hillhead, Rossnagalliagh which was quite close to the school; about fifty yards away. He walked to school and wore corduroy trousers and a jersey. When Paddy was at Rossnagalliagh the teachers' names were Mrs Gull, (maybe Gill), Mrs Elliott and Miss Reynalds. They taught 130-140 pupils in one room and the children sat in long desks which reached from one end of the room to the other. The curriculum included history, reading and writing. The children's homework may have included sums and spellings.

At playtime the children had very little space within the school walls and as a result played on the main Strabane-Londonderry road. In later years the children used an old barn to have their lunch in the middle of the day but when Paddy attended one of the teachers, (the principal?), kept her coal and her pony there.

The school day lasted from 9:00am until 3:00 pm. The school was closed for six weeks holiday's in the summer.

L-R: Kate, Maggie and Rebecca McCorkell

Below is an example of a family who attended Rossnagalliagh between 1916-1918.

Rebecca or Becky, Maggie and Katie McCorkell and their brother James came over the fields from the townland of Drumcorkin to Rossnagalliagh School. The family moved quite regularly and was later to live at Tully Bridge. Their father (Willy) was a labourer on Thompson's farm in Cloghogle, near Bready Co Tyrone and mother (Martha) was a dressmaker. Mrs McCorkell would probably have made the children's school clothes as well as dressmaking for the local community.

The additional money earned by women such as Mrs McCorkell, therefore, would probably have been very important to the family income. Unlike some children of the period, however, their parents were able to afford hobnail boots which the children wore to school and to Sunday school.

CHAPTER 6

THE NEW NORTHERN IRELAND AND INTER- WAR YEARS

After the setting up of the Northern Ireland state in 1921 the school came under the Ministry of Education and was called a Public Elementary School, rather than a National School, due to the Education Act of 1923. It was to be a maintained or voluntary school.

Picture Above: Mrs McColgan on right c1921/2

Piture on the left: Miss Candy on left

Miss Candy on left c 1923 unknown teacher on right.
All the children seem to be enjoying the moment. Note some are bare footed.
Front row- l to r: third child ?King, fourth ?Kelly, last on right Thomas Gillespie,
Second row l to r: sixth child Grace Kilgore, eleventh child Jim Cassidy,
Third row l to r: second child ?Gillespie, fifth John McGrory, sixth Sam Browne,
eighth John Kelly, ninth Charlie Cassidy
Fifth row r to l: Lily Browne, Mary Toland
Back Row l to r: third child Jeannie McCorkell, fifth Lily Gillespie

Pupils

The pupils attending Rossnaglliagh in this period came from the following areas:-
Newbuildings, Quay Lane, Dam Row, Newbuildings Street (the main Strabane
–Londonderry Road), Primity, Victoria Bridge, Magheracannon, Clampernow,
Gortin, Prehen-Golf Links, Rossnagalliagh, Hillhead, Burndennet, Magheramason,
Upper and Lower Tully, Drumcorkin, Ballyorr, and Dunhugh.

Between 1923 and 1934, 83 Roman Catholic, 54 Presbyterian, 16 Church of Ireland
and one Methodist pupil attended. From 1933-37 the average number of children
at the school was 55 with approx 43 attending on a regular basis.

The rolls in 1930's also reveal that a substantial number were to attend Rossnagalliagh
only for a short period, or came from other schools, as the family of labourers
probably moved regularly to find work.

The farmers in the 1930's were affected by falling food prices and this resulted in few employing full -time workers. Labourer's wages, therefore, were as low as £1 5s 0d to £1 7s 6d, less than the £1 10s 0d a married man and two children received on the "dole." The Depression between 1931 and 1939, however, affected all sectors and many were completely dependent on state benefits.[1]

Staff changes and Inspector's Reports

By 1921 the Board decided that Mrs Elliott could retire and that on 30th June her salary would be withdrawn. However retirement seems to have been put on hold for a year as Mr Beamish, School Inspector, visiting on 14th and 15th February, 1922 reported,

"The Principal retires very shortly evidently after a long and successful career. Because of the activity of her daughter, the assistant, she does only a limited share of the work at present, but a good diligent spirit is preserved and proficiency is pretty sound in general".

Nevertheless he also stated that "Infant oral training is a matter which calls for extra attention and drawing needs sustained care and development. More can be done, too, to popularise singing in the upper groups".

Mrs Elliott was found to be a "highly efficient" teacher while her daughter, now Mrs McColgan, was "efficient. "

Mrs Elliott retired on 31st May 1922; she had taught for 45 years. She received her pension of £101 11s a year from 12th July 1922 which was later raised to £125. 15s 8d.

On 21st May, 1923 a Mr J H Tibbs, School Inspector, indicated that the school had been "under the charge of three Principals in succession".

Mrs McColgan therefore had taken over as Principal from her mother for only a short period, between June 1922 and March 1923, when a Miss Anna M. Candy was appointed Principal and Mary J McCloskey as an assistant. The rolls show that members of the McColgan family were born at this time and this may explain Mrs McColgan's absence as Principal.

From L. to R: Mrs Elliott, Miss Candy and Mrs McColgan.

Miss Candy was 29 years old.She lived in Mill Street, Waterside and past pupils recall that she travelled to school on a small motorbike.

In 1923 the Inspector found Miss Candy was "doing useful work" but warned that "schemes in all subjects should now be made out and better daily preparation is needed". The Assistant teacher however, was not reaching the standard expected by the Inspector and he recommended that she should "improve her organisation, discipline and methods so as to attain more satisfactory results in the Junior division". The Inspector also noted that the school required a map of the world, a globe, 3 blackboards and 3 easels.

Miss Candy and a new assistant, Rebecca Hegarty, were assessed as "efficient" at the next Inspector's visit on 11th February 1924. A Mr A Thompson inspected the school again on 13th March 1924 and reported, "Promising work is being done in this school. The pupils in standards 3 and 4 show a good deal of trained intelligence and are as a rule bright and alert. Writing and mental arithmetic require more efficient teaching in the junior standards and reading should be more fluent distinct and expressive.The infants are intelligent and appear to be making good progress."

However, he found those in Standard 5 had not attended well and this was affecting their work. Attendance of older children particularly remained a problem as they may have been required to help in the home or farm, or earn much needed additional income.

Mr Thompson called again on 22nd November 1924 and wrote,

"Considering the period of the school year the answering of the pupils was on the whole quite good. Mental arithmetic needs working up in the senior standards. Order and discipline are very good and the children are carefully trained in the habits of neatness, politeness, etc".

At the visit of Inspector, Mr N. G. N. Anderson, on 22nd September 1926 the report showed that "the two teachers (Miss Candy and Miss Hegarty) who are engaged in the one small room of this school, do satisfactory work."

The Principal's class had answered readily and worked well under examination, however spelling needed attention in Standard 3-4, and arithmetic was "weak in regard to mental work". The junior classes were generally receiving "satisfactory training in the subjects of their course but Standard 1 pupils should be further advanced in their programme in arithmetic".

Once again the School Inspector was impressed by the children's behaviour and order in the classroom as he ended his report by commenting, "The tone of the school merits praise. The pupils receive a very good training in habits of politeness and orderly conduct". [2]

By 1928 Mrs McColgan had replaced Miss Candy as Principal and was joined by an assistant, Miss Josephine Campbell. There were also to be a number of substitute teachers between 1929 and 1937, including Bella McIlhinney from April –July 1929; Rosaleen Lynch October 1930; Shelia Coyle January 1931-April 1931; Teresa J Hegarty April 1933; Kathleen Muldoon July 1933, Teresa J Hegarty October 1933; Mary Cunningham 1934, Agnes McFadden July –October 1937; Kathleen McCormick October 1937.

By 1924, the new Ministry of Education had taken over the Board's role of providing grants on a monthly basis towards the teacher's salaries. For example on 14th January 1928 the grant towards part of the Principal's monthly salary was £17 16s 10d and her assistant was £12 16s.0d, and on 13th June 1929 the Principal salary was £20 11s 2d and assistant remained at £12 16s. 0d. On13[th] July, 1930 the Principal received £20 14s 5d and her assistant £12. 16s.(see end of chapter for all grants between January 1928 - August 1930).

Along with being partly funded by local and central government, the Irish Society was to continue to supplement the teacher's salary by £15, plus the cost of heating and insuring the school after the transfer.

Rules and the Curriculum

In 1929 Rossnagalliagh was given direction from the Ministry of Education for keeping the rolls. Teachers were to ensure that no under fours were at the school and no child under seven in the infant class. This rule, however, does not seem to have been complied with at any stage in the school.

Boys under seven were not to be enrolled where there was no mistress, unless there was no local school with a mistress available, and in the eighth year there were to be no boys in the girls' class. The rule about having no boys in the girls' class was not adhered to, but would have been impossible to keep at Rossnagalliagh due to the lack of space.

Secular education was to be taught for not less than four hours, five days a week, with not more than one hour interval (usually children had half an hour break for something to eat in the middle of the day from 12:30 pm to 11:00 pm). School started not later than 10:30 am to 11:00 am and in summer not later than 10:00 am until 3:30 pm.

In 1923 the new Ministry of Education had decided that the number of compulsory subjects was to be reduced, and one practical subject such as domestic economy, nature study, horticulture or woodwork to be included. For example, the Infant Grade could be taught speaking, reading, numbers, singing, games and "educational handwork".

Irish history was also on the curriculum of schools as shown by Maggie McCorkell's book dated November 1924. The book was called "A Child's Story of Ireland." by A. B. Ochiltree Ferguson produced by the Educational Company of Ireland Ltd.

The chapters included:-
In the Olden Time; The tales of the Bards; St Patrick; St Columba; Brian Boru; The Coming of the Normans; The Siege at Waterford;: The Faithful Norman; Edward the Bruce; Aodh O'Neill; Aodh O'Donnell; The two Aodhs; The Battle of Yellow Ford; Benburb; King James and King William; The Battle of the Boyne; The Seige of Athlone; (and the second Siege of Athlone); Patrick Sarsfield; The Siege and Treaty of Limerick; How England Broke the Treaty; Henry Grattan; The Volunteers; The United Irishmen; Wolfe Tone and The Union.

We have no record of what form geography lessons took but examples of examination questions below taken from Birdstown National School, Co. Donegal may have been similar to that in Rossnagalliagh :-

Grade 2 and 3 - What and where are:- The Arctic, France, Tasmania, Japan, Egypt, Petrograd and Paris?

Grade 4 - Give length, breadth, area, population and length of the coastline of Ireland?

Grade 5-8 -What do you know of Brest, Cherbourg, Waterloo, Utrecht, Zurich, Rome, Pola, Varna, Corfu, Petrograd, Adjaccio, Nicholaieu, Rochefort, Copenhagen, Magdeburg and Hamburg?

The questions show children as young as six or seven, in Grade 2, were expected to have not only a local, but a worldwide geographic knowledge.

By May, 1925 senior pupils could have entered for an Elementary School Certificate which replaced the National Educational Higher Grade Certificate. Passing the Certificate enabled pupils to go to Secondary or Technical College without having to do an entrance exam. In 1932 the Certificate included English, geography, arithmetic and drawing as compulsory subjects. However only around 1,000 pupils were entered for the examination and 831 passed, and there are no indications that the pupils at Rossnagalliagh were entered. [3]

Senior girls were to continue to be taught how to sew and knit but by 1923 the cookery classes had been discontinued for a year and a year later the situation had not improved. The Inspector noted that this was due to Rossnaglliagh being a "mixed school and there was no room". However accounts given by past pupils show that cookery was once again on the syllabus by 1929 taught by Mrs McColgan. A small cookery class was still on the curriculum in May 1935 as the following items were requested from the Board:-

2 rolling pins, 2 large bowls, 1 large lined saucepan, 1 boiler to heat washing water, 2 pudding bowls. [4]

c 1932 Miss Josephine Campbell on right
Front row l to r: James Kerr, Myrtle Goodwin, Kathleen Smith, Maureen Ferry,
Tom McColgan, John Crumley
Second Row l to r: Angela McColgan, Mabel Monteith, Jeannie Falconer, Kathleen Mitchell,
Jeannie Phillips, Sue Phillips
Third Row l to r: Sarah (Sadie) Smith, Sean Ferry, Tommy Thompson, Maggie Crumley, ?
Fourth Row l to r: Laurence King, Pat Kelly, Francie Hone, Sam Mitchell, John Devine, Willie Falconer

Interestingly, in 1933, needlework would have been available for boys in 1st and 2nd Grade but boys at Rossnagalliagh are not recorded to have been given the opportunity. Nor did senior boys receive horticulture classes, unlike boys of the same age at other local schools, such as Bready School. This was probably due to the lack of space around the School and that there was no male teacher to instruct them.

By the end of the 1930's the number of school examinations were greatly reduced compared to those undertaken by pupils earlier in the century, as can be seen in the example below.

Isobel King began school on 30th June 1939, aged 6. Unlike pupils in the late 19th Century she did not do any examinations in Infant class. In 1stGrade she did reading, writing, composition, arithmetic, drawing and vocal music, and in 2nd Grade, in 1942, she sat the same examinations. There are no further examinations recorded until she left in 1945, aged 13. Isobel received full marks for all the examinations she undertook.

Problems Inside and Outside School

Mrs McColgan was to inherit the overcrowding problem when she returned to her post as Principal. Overcrowded classrooms were not only to hinder adequate room to teach and learn, but also continued to increase the possibility of epidemics, such as measles, and in February 1929 an influenza epidemic was to close the school once again.

On 3rd December 1927 the question of additional accommodation was again raised, and on 22nd June 1928 proposed alterations to provide accommodation by converting the teacher's residence into classrooms was raised, and approved. Mrs McColgan and her family, therefore, were to move out of the school building to Upper Burndennet, near Strabane. She had lived in the school rent free until this point. The school's Daily Report Books 1927-33 verify that the teacher no longer had a free residence in the school. By December 1930 an Inspector's report shows that the school rooms were enlarged, new floors laid and new windows and doors installed. [5]

Pupils Kathleen Hamilton nee McCracken (1939-46) and George McLaughlin (1945-52) recalled the school now included an upper room for the older children and a lower one for the younger classes. In reality both rooms were either side of the front door of the school.

The bigger room was 31 ft long and 16ft in breadth, and 10.ft 6inches in height and the smaller room was 19 ft 6 inches long, 16 ft broad and 10ft 6inches high according to the Daily Report book of 1933-1938. These measurements indicate that any changes made to the rooms to accommodate the Principal and her family over the years were simply reversed.

Miss Campbell on left and Mrs McColgan on right c 1932
Front row l to r: ? Hugh Gillespie, John O'Donnell, Maggie Crumley, Maureen Ferry,
Sam McNeely, Jim McColgan, Sean Ferry, Terence Brown, James Kerr, Willie Falconer,
Jim Hamilton, Laurence King, Sue Phillips
Second Row l to r: Harry King. Jeannie Phillips, Mamie Brown, Myrtle Reid, Sarah Falconer, Kathleen Kerr,
Jeannie Falconer, Sheena Quigg, Angela McColgan, Rita O'Donnell, Jeannie Monteith, Margaret Kerr,
Mable Monteith, John Devine
Third Row l to r: Hammy Jamieson, Tony Devine, ? Sam Mitchell, Iris Jackson, May King, Rosemary Eakin,
Mary Kelly, Isobel Henry, Rose Phillips, Violet Monteith, Ellen Brown
Fourth Row L to r: Corny McCloskey, Andy McNeely, Danny Gillespie, John McColgan, Francie O'Donnell,
Charlie O'Donnell, Bertie King, Lexie Mills

The heating for the classrooms were provided by a free standing stove and an open fire. James Robinson recalled bringing turf for the fire in 1937-45 and coal being gathered from the road if it had been spilled by the coalman visiting a neighbouring house. Whins were used to light the fire.

The question of heating the school rooms, however, was not without controversy. An Inspector who had called on 11th March 1926 had found three pupils had procured the key and had proceeded to light the fire. He reported that the situation "was highly dangerous in the absence of the teacher".

The inspector had found the teacher who came from Derry by bus (Miss Campbell?) had not arrived until 10.00am when religious instruction should have started at 9:30am – 10:00am, and then roll call at 10:10am. However the situation had not changed in the following years when we read Mary King's account of lighting the fire while she was at school.

Nevertheless, there was a lack of warmth inside the school rooms as pupils had to wear their coats in the winter time, and looked forward to going up near the teacher's desk as the fire was behind it, (see Kathleen Hamilton's account). Cold weather, such as frost in 1935 or a blizzard in 1937, resulted in the school closing altogether.

Although the overcrowding problem had been dealt with, on 26th November 1931 the request of desks for the junior pupils was to be raised again. The Inspectors report shows that "at least nine modern dual desks (should) be provided for juniors at an early date". However, two years later, on 21st February 1933, the Inspector again asked that the manager give the "question of desks for juniors his early attention". At this time there were only 8 desks each 9 ft, 4 desks at 12 ft and one form at 5 ft for the 63 pupils attending.

Example of a dual desk with ink wells

Finally on 12th December 1933 the Inspector confirmed that the dual desks had arrived and that the school is "now fully equipped with suitable desks". In the Daily Report Book February1933-38, the number of desks included 14 dual desks, 3 large desks, 3 small desks and 1 form of 5 ft. In the Report Book 1938-43, 27 desks are recorded at 3 ft 4 inches long.

Outside, the cloakroom and outoffices were given attention by 1930 after the manager proposed to have new ones built at a suitable distance from the school house. Improvements such as this came under the 1930 Act and grants of 65% of the cost were now available to schools such as Rossnagalliagh for running costs, new buildings or reconstruction; although in the Daily Report Book of 1933-38 there is a comment that "no evidence of grants (were) made by Ministry of Education or Local Authority ".[5]

The "dry" toilets which were provided meant that they did not flush as there was no access to mains water. Ellen McGarrigle nee Brown (1929-1935) remembered the new purpose built toilet at the rear of the school had two toilets side by side with wooden seats.

Problems in the Playground

The ongoing problem of lack of space for the children to play was again to be raised on 8th October 1924 when the Inspector stated the obvious, "there is no playground except a small space in front so that the children are on the main road at imminent risk".

By this period traffic had increased on the road and this might have focused those responsible on the need to act. However the problem was not to be dealt with in 1924, and was therefore raised again on a visit by the Inspector in 1926 when he recorded that, "the danger to pupils on the road is great". Five years later on a visit by the Inspector, dated 24th January1931, the Manager was again asked to give his immediate attention to the situation. Personal accounts show a playground was finally available at the back of the school by the end of the 1930's, where the boys played football, however, the girls continued to play in the small space at the front.

Accidents were, unfortunately, to happen within the new playground as in July 1935 a boy was injured by a missile at playtime. The Ministry apologised to the child's father but no action was taken against the staff. However it was noted that missiles were to be "strongly discouraged."

The need for adequate supervision of the children at playtime was another feature of the Inspector's reports. In October 1924 he had found the pupils "were not under supervision during play". In fact he had found two pupils had gone away from school and had not returned for 45 minutes after they should have been in class. The Inspector provided suggestions for appropriate supervision during lunch time.[7]

Lunch in this period had to be eaten on forms provided in an outside shed, situated just within the school wall, but beside the main road. As a result it may have been tempting to slip outside the school wall when the teacher was not looking!

Most children were to bring a "lunch" to eat in the middle of the school day which, for some, may have consisted of bread and butter and a drink of water from the pump at the back of the school. James Robinson, (1937-45) however, recalled that many children had little to eat when he was at Rossnagalliagh, and when one pupil had dinner brought to the school by her mother, anything she left was eagerly finished by the other children. Some pupils have memories of eating turnips on their way home as they had nothing to eat all day.

Pupils' welfare

Although most families in the area had access to a small plot of land or kept a pig or poultry, the close relationship between poverty, unemployment and sickness was a reality across Northern Ireland. Pneumonia and tuberculosis was to kill 49% of 15-25 years old and life expectancy in 1931 was 57.1 years. [8]

Inadequate health care and lack of hygiene also added to the problem and resulted in many deaths under 15 years old from infectious diseases such as influenza, whooping cough or measles. As a precaution Rossnagalliagh closed due to a whooping cough epidemic in July and September 1935.

However a third of a pint of milk was provided by the Government for all school pupils after the wartime blitz of 1941. The Government in Northern Ireland had been forced to act as a result of many evacuated children having being found to be ill nourished. Children thereafter paid full price or half price for the milk, or it was provided free for those who could not afford it. In some schools the teacher had to measure the milk out of a churn but bottles were available in Rossnagalliagh.

School children at primary level were also to benefit from the attentions of the school nurse. She examined the children's hair for lice, their eyesight, ears and teeth and investigated general skin infections.

James Robinson recalled the annual visit from the nurse prior to the onset of the new Health Service in July 1948. He particularly remembers one boy who was asked by the nurse to take off his shirt and jumper for an examination and proceeded to take off layers of shirts in the process to the amusement of the class. (James remembered about 12 shirts although this may have been a few too many for any boy to own at that time.)

1   Bardon, p547
    Government Grants to the Principal and assistant in Report Book for years 1927-33
    are as follows:-
    1928-14th Jan £17 16s 10d and £12 16s 0d14[th] Feb   £18 0s 0d and £11. 0s 0d 14th
    March £18.0s 0 and £11 0s 0d
    14[th]April £24. 6s 6d and £16 8s 0d 14th May £18 0s 0d and £11 0s 0d 13th June £18
    0s 0d and £11 0s 0d
    13th July £ £18 4s 9d –no assistant pay 13th August £ 18 0s 0d and £10 0s 0d
    13[th]Sept £18 0s 0d and £11 0s 0d
    13th Oct £17 18s 6d and £13 8s 4d13[th] Nov £18 0s 0d and £11 0s 0d 13th Dec £18
    0s 0d and £11 0s 0d
    192913th Jan £22 11s 2d and £12 16s 0d 13th Feb £18 0s 0d and £11 0s 0d
    13th March £18 0s 0d and £11 0s 0d 13th April £42 0s 0d and £12 16s 0d 13th May
    £18 0s 0d and £11. 0s 0d
    13th June £18 0s 0d and £11 0s 0d13[th] July £20 11s 2d and £12 16s 0d 13th August
    £19 0s 0d and £11 0s 0d
    13[th]Sept £19 0s 0d and £11 0s 0d13[th] Oct £20 11s 2d and £12 16s 0d13[th] Dec £19
    0s 0d and £11 0s 0d
    193013th Jan £20 11s 2d and £12 16s 0d 13th Feb £19 0s 0d and £11 0s 0d 13th
    March £19 0s 0d and £11 0s 0d
    13th April £20 14s 5d and £12 16s 0d 13th May £20 0s 0d and £11 0s 0d 13th June
    £20 0s 0d and £11 0s 0d
    13th July £20 14 5d and £12 16s 0d 13th august £20 0s 0d and £11 0s 0d
2   PRONI ED/4/E/15
3   History of Irish Education, p180
4   PRONI ED/6/3/5/1
5   Ibid
6   Ibid
7   ibid
8   Bardon, P531,532

Personal recollections

Mrs Ellen (Eleanor) McGarrigle (nee Brown)1929-1938   lived off Woodside Road, along the side of the Golf Links, in a house belonging to her uncle. She gave an interview in March 2011. She was 90 years old. Her father was a greenkeeper at Rosemount Bowling Green.

Ellen started school when she was seven years old as her parents thought it was too far for a younger child to walk on her own. As she was the oldest in the family she was to be in charge of her sisters Mabel (called Mamie) and Sarah, and brothers Billy and Lexie, when they went to school, even carrying the youngest brother on her back when he was tired walking up the hill home.

Her parents were very particular about their children's appearance. Her father boiled ivy leaves and, with the strained water brushed her school gym frock if it was stained, and hung it up to dry. Ellen wore a blouse with her gym frock in summer and a jumper under it in the winter. Her clothes were shop bought. In summer she wore tan coloured sandals with cream rubber soles and in winter wore wellingtons. She remembered that some children did not have any shoes or boots at all. She carried a small case to school, instead of a school bag, for her books.

Ellen sat beside Terence Brown, from Hillhead, whom she thinks was an only child, and was taught by Miss Campbell, who was in charge of the younger pupils at this time.

Ellen recalled first thing in the morning the Catholic children had a prayer while Protestant children waited in the kitchen. There was also an extra half hour at the end of the day when the Catholic children would have had religious instruction, while the Protestant children went home.

Subjects included arithmetic, geography, composition and English, and homework may have consisted of tables and spellings.

Mrs McColgan taught needlework to the older pupils. Ellen recalled making a petticoat with a lace edge. Her mother had bought the material in the town. Ellen also had cookery classes with Mrs McColgan, and wore a white apron. She made milk puddings and buns with ingredients she had brought from home. She did not take the results of the cookery class home, but gave them to another pupil called

Example of a map of Ireland found in schools of the period.

Sam McNeely. Sam and Ellen were to remain friends throughout their lives, as did many other pupils who had attended Rossnagalliagh.

Ellen remembered that there were two classrooms at the school. One room was on the left and the other was on the right of the entrance of the school. There were large glossy maps of the world on the walls of the classroom. The rooms were heated by a fire in the younger children's class and a stove in the "upper" older children's class. The children brought kindling and the fires burnt coke, which lasted all day.

At the back of the school were the dry toilets in a separate building. The toilets had two lavatory basins beside each other with wooden seats.

At the entrance to the school was a rough shed where the children ate their lunches of bread and milk. Ellen did not think the school provided milk at that time. A couple of forms (benches) were provided, but there was not enough room for all the children to sit down. The children played at the back and front of the school- the boys played marbles and the girls skipped or played ball games. Ellen did not play at lunch time as her mother had warned her to look after her brothers. She did not have to take the same care of her sisters!

A nurse came to the school and tested the children's eyesight. Ellen recalled an influenza epidemic in the area which resulted in the school closing.

However Ellen does not remember any visitors coming to the school, as anyone who called was not introduced to the children. Ellen considered Mrs McColgan to have been a very good teacher. She left school when she was 15 and did not do any examinations before leaving.

Mrs McColgan on right c 1934
Front row l to r: Kathleen Kerr, Ellen Brown, Terence Browne, Maggie Callan, Rosie Phillips,   ? ,
Jeannie Falconer, Jeannie Monteith, (not seated) Mamie Brown,
Second Row l to r ? , Callan Sheen Quigg, Margo McColgan, Maggie Hone, Sara Falconer, Mary Kelly,
Third Row l to r: Sam Devine, Jim McColgan, ? , Sam McNeely, Harry King,
Back Row l to r: ? Henry, Sam Mitchell, Tony Devine, ? , John McColgan, ?

CHAPTER 7

DURING THE SECOND WORLD WAR AND 1945-1950

The children attending school during the Second World War came from Magheracannon, Lifford, Primity, Ballyorr, Rossnagalliagh, Tully Bridge, Newbuildings, Newbuildings Street, Dam Row, Quay Lane, Donemana Road, the Railway Station at Newbuildings, Gortin, Coolmaghery, Magheramason, Gortmesson, Tamnakerry and Gortinure. A limited number of children came from Londonderry after houses in the city were hit by a bomb in 1941 leaving 150 homeless.

Between 1935-49 the religious make up of the children were as follows- 107 Roman Catholic, 61 Presbyterian and 54 Church of Ireland pupils. There were no Methodist pupils in this period.

Impact of War

During the war the children were fitted with gas masks which they had to carry to and from school. However it is unclear if there were any adjustments to the school building, such as taping the windows against air raids, but it unlikely as generally there were few precautions taken by the Government prior to the raid in 1941.

Although there was no conscription, pupils whose fathers were farmers and labourers were exempt from enlisting as they were needed for the war effort. The number of labourers had begun to fall in Ulster by 1930's due in part to the rise of family run farms, but this is not reflected in the Rossnagalliagh area where the majority of pupils' fathers were still recorded as agricultural labourers. The growth of flax and increase in crops during the war years had provided a major boost and created work.

This may explain why there is almost no unemployment shown in the school rolls available, although most were not full time workers and the need to find work still resulted in children having to move from one school to another. For example, the McClelland, Boyd and Rutherford families who came to live in Rossnagalliagh from Creeve in Co. Donegal.

The parents of the Boyd children had been employed in the dairy and as a labourer on the farm of John Roulston in Donegal in 1930's, and were reunited when the

Roulstons came to farm in Rossnagalliagh in 1940. The Roulstons also employed men from Gibraltar whose families had come to live at a camp at Tagherina, and, later in the war, German prisoners, some of whom tried to escape.[1]

It is also vital to make mention of the fishing industry which played a very important economic role in the Newbuildings area as it would have augmented the wages of labouring families from May to August. During the war, work in the docks at Londonderry increased dramatically and this also provided much needed extra income. Mothers, such as Mrs McCracken of Newbuildings, also played their part as they were employed as dressmaker for the locality.

In the 1940's many pupils at rural schools helped the family income by gathering potatoes. Pupils would have been hired by local farmers who, by 1937, owned their own land, usually between 15-50 acres. This resulted in children not attending school for long periods and was probably to force the Education Authorities to give an official annual potato- gathering holiday during October. However winter conditions continued to ensure a sharp drop in attendance, for example in December 1944, 33 pupils out of a total of 75 were present.

During the war a limited number of fathers in the Newbuildings area were to be involved with the armed forces. Those who enlisted sent letters and photographs home which was to have an impact on school life. For example, George McLaughlin (1945-52) recalled being very familiar with places, such as Hong Kong, Palestine and Baghdad, which he was able to share with the class in geography lessons as his father was in the RAF, and his uncle, George Phillips, was in the Army.

Past pupils also joined up, such as brothers Maurice and Irwin Reid of Lower Tully (1927) who were in the RAF, and David McCorkell of Primity (1921) who was in the Burma Rifles. It is claimed that when Irwin returned to his home at Clampernow bonfires were lit to welcome him home. Unfortunately his brother Maurice, who was a pilot, was shot down over France in February 1944.

Some fathers, such as those of the McClelland, Boyd and Roulston children of Rossnagalliagh, joined the home guard as did past pupils Jack McCorkell (1916) of Primity, Willy Lecky (1931) from Coolmaghery and James Falconer (1929) from Upper Tully.

Terence Brown of Hillhead, (1929) had joined the Royal Navy and returned in uniform to the school in 1946 where he impressed the children with his war stories. Another visitor to the school on 2nd July 1946 was Squadron Leader Reverend McShane. Their visits may have coincided with a sports day which was held to celebrate the end of the war.

Teaching Staff, Salaries and Changes in Education

Winifred Foley (nee Reid) who had been a substitute teacher from January 1936, became the new assistant in 1940, replacing Josephine Campbell. Substitutes in this period included Mary J McCullagh 1942, Margaret McMullan April 1943 and Mary Donnelly in January 1944.

In 1943 the Ministry gave a grant towards the Principal and her assistant's salary which included a war bonus. The Principal's salary on 13th April was £22 12s 4d and a capitation grant of £22 14s 4d which meant the total monthly salary was £45 6s 8d. On 13th May the Principal's grant was £22. 0s 0d, plus a war bonus of £7 and her assistant's was £12 12s 5d, plus a war bonus of £9. On 13th June the Principal's grant was £21 6s 8d and on 17th July £19.12s 4d.The grant to the teachers seems not to have increased much from late 1920s and early 1930's.

The Ministry of Education also proposed an increase in capital grants to Catholic schools for heating, cleaning and maintenance from 60% to 100%. Money was also available for free milk, lunches and schoolbooks to the less well off.

In 1946 wrangling over the Education Bill was to divide politicians and the churches, but the reforms which were being discussed also included converting Elementary schools into Primary schools, and introducing Secondary schools. Pupils could thereafter leave Primary schools at eleven after selection by a qualifying examination. The most able 20% would go to Grammar schools while the remaining 80% would go to Intermediate or Further Education College. In 1947 two children at Rossnagalliagh undertook the first test and passed which delighted Mrs McColgan. (see Kathleen Hamilton's account).

It was hoped that these reforms would reduce class sizes. However, many of the children remained at Rossnagalliagh until they left to go to work at 14. The school leaving age had been proposed to be raised to 15, but due to "logistical problems of implementing the far reaching reforms" (i.e. the new Education system) it was not adopted until 1950's.

School Books

Although new ideas on education were being introduced at Rossnagalliagh, some things remained the same. Vere Foster copy books continued to be used to help pupils form their letters, mottoes or quotations such as "many men of many minds" and learning by rote was thought to ensure pupils knew their tables and ABC. The infant class also continued to use slate and chalk. When the pupils had been promoted to writing on paper in the early days of the school they may have used quill pens, which could have been made by the teacher, but Kathleen Hamilton recalled the pupils during the war years used utility pencils and poor quality writing materials.

Noleen McColgan (daughter of the Principal) who attended the school in 1940's was regularly sent to Strabane for school books by her mother as the Board did not supply all that was necessary. An example of the kind used at Rossnagalliagh was the Viaduct Exercise Book shown below belonging to Rosemary McLaughlin.

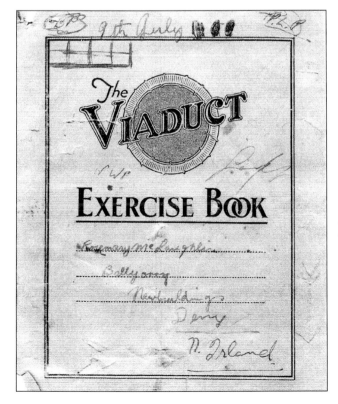

On the left:
Example of an exercise book in 1940's

Reading material for the younger pupils in this period included Lily Bradley's (1944-55) book, shown below, which was called "Through the Garden Gate" by Mabel O'Donnell and Rona Munro. It was a book in the Janet and John series.

The chapters included Betsy-Lee, Little Goat, John finds Janet, Chicken-Licken, At the farm, Little Red Hen, Peter and Darky, Little Jack Rabbit, The Toy Mender, Little Ant. A vocabulary of over 200 words can be found in the book which may have been used for spellings or help with compositions.

Reading book used in 1940-50's

The book's contents clearly shows the enormous difference between the subject material thought suitable for reading in primary schools in 1940's compared to Maggie McCorkell's book in the 1920's.

In 1948-58 Charlotte Temple's nee McLaughlin's arithmetic book was called "Daily Life Arithmetic" by Browne and Nolan Ltd. This was designed to reflect everyday life and its problems. It shows the approximate price of food at that time, the inclusion of tobacco on grocery lists, but not cigarettes, and the wages of "servants". Girls leaving Rosnagalliagh may still have found work "in service" in the late 1940's. (see Kathleen Hamilton's account.)

Below are some arithmetic "problems" from the book:-
"If a man smokes 4 ozs of tobacco a week how many lbs would he smoke in 16 weeks?

Your mother bought 2 quarts of milk on Sunday and from Monday to Saturday 3 pints daily. The milk was 3 ¾ d per pint.

(a) How much did she pay for 7 days milk?

(b) What quantity in gallons and quarts did she buy?

Your mother asks you to find out how much she will have to pay for these goods-

1stone of sugar at 4 ½ d per lb
1¾ lbs of tea at 2s 8d per lb.
6 eggs at 2s 3d a dozen
¼ lb of tobacco at 1s1d an oz
2½ lbs of butter at 1s 6d per lb
Make out the bill she may expect to receive.

A servant is paid £26 yearly: how much will she earn in 3½ months?

1. Roulston, Roulstons of Donegal, 1998

Personal Recollections

Mrs Sadie McMorris (née Boyd) attended school 1930-39.

Sadie came to Rossnagalliagh to live from Creeve, Co Donegal. She had attended Crossroads National School in Co Donegal before coming to Rossnagalliagh School, along with her brothers, John, Jim, Bertie and David and sister Violet. Other pupils in Sadie's class were Terence Browne, John and Phil Donnell, the Campbells from Magheramason and the Brownes from Rossnagalliiagh.

Miss Campbell and Mrs. McColgan were to be her new teachers at Rossnagalliagh. Sadie thought Rossnagalliagh provided a good education due to Mrs. McColgan's very varied curriculum, compared to Crossroads School where the family had learnt "the basics".

The curriculum at Rossnagalliagh included arithmetic, geography, English, composition, poetry, painting, singing, drawing, needlework, cookery and PE, which included some dancing. Pupils' paintings were displayed on the classroom wall. Sadie enjoyed needlework best, and made a "Shirley Temple" dress for a young child. Mrs. McColgan took Sadie for cookery, and Maureen Ferry and Maggie Kelly were also in the cookery class. Maggie was Sadie's pal.

She does not remember the teacher having to use the cane, but some boys may have had to be punished.

There was no milk for the children at this time, but at dinner break Sadie went home as the family lived very close to the school. The rest of the children took lunch in a shed inside the school gate. It was a stone building. She thought there was another small shed at the rear of the school, near the toilets.

Sadie wore dresses and sandals in the summer and skirts and jumpers in the winter. She considered that the coal fires in the two classrooms kept the pupils warm in winter, while the rooms were cool in summer.

Sadie did not remember any visitors to the school, but thought an inspector might have come. It was a happy school -one big family. The children looked after each other. Sadie left school when she was 14 years old to work in Kennedy's Factory in Magazine Street, Londonderry. She enjoyed her work. The family came to Foyle Crescent in 1953.

James Robinson attended the school 1937-45.

James and his brother David and sisters Joyce, Vina and Iris had originally attended Bready School and then came to Rossnagalliagh in 1937 from Killymallaght School, which James had attended only a matter of months. James believed that the family changed schools due to a disagreement over punishment by the master of Killymallaght. They lived at Gortin, at a place called McCullagh's Corner. The family were sometimes late for school in winter as they had quite a distance to come and James recalled Mrs. McColgan's displeasure when they arrived after the school day had started. The Principal was not too pleased with him also when he hid in the school cupboard.

There were three teachers at the school, but Mrs. McColgan had moved to Burndennet, and travelled to school by bus with her children. The cleaner at the school was Hannah Toland who lit the fire and opened the school. The caretakers during the war were Mrs W Gillespie, mother of one of the children, and Mrs Browne. Mr Joe King may have been caretaker from 1944-52. James took turf to school for the fire and coal from the roadside if the coal man had dropped any.

He recalls the McLaughlin children from Lower Tully, Rosemary Collins, the McCracken children from Newbuildings Street and Colleen McEleney came to the school at that time. James thought that Colleen's mother may have brought dinner to the school for her as they lived close by. As there were no school dinners James remembered many of the children had very little to eat. Some would have eaten raw turnips out of a field on the way home.

When he left school James worked in Crawford's Chemist in the Waterside, then Leckpatrick Creamery and finally joined the Army. James was to see many countries while in the Army and he recalls serving in the Suez Crisis.

Kathleen Hamilton (née McCracken) attended from October 1939-January 1946. Kathleen wrote the following piece

"My memories of Rossnagalliagh School"
When my family came to live in Newbuildings in October 1939 Rossnagalliagh was the nearest school to the village. I was five and a half years old and had been to school in Clandeboy Estate in Bangor where we came from, so my mother was

anxious to get me started as soon as possible. She made a few enquiries from the people in the village as Rossnagalliagh was mainly a Catholic School and found out that they taught both religions which was great for us. One of the senior girls, her name was Maud Phillips, took my mother and me the first day and introduced us to Mrs. McColgan, the head mistress. After that Maudie, as she was called, took me every day until I could go on my own. We all had to walk to school so there was always five or six of us together. It took about half an hour to walk to school. We had to walk together in all kinds of weather. It was rare for children to miss a day from school.

There were just the two class rooms - the lower and upper rooms, as we called them and two teachers. Mrs. McColgan was the head teacher and she taught the older pupils from about eight years old upwards in the upper room. The lower room was infants and senior infants and first and second class as they were called then. The teacher was Miss Winifred Reid who later became Mrs. Foley. Between the two classrooms, the total children on the roll would have been around 100. Fellow pupils included Kathleen Gillespie, Collette McColgan and Betty Ferry. She (Miss Foley) used to take us for PE exercises which were done outside in good weather. We enjoyed the break from ordinary lessons. But if you were behind in some of your work you didn't get going out.

It was wartime while I was there and we didn't have any school meals, just a piece of bread or two slices of bread put together with jam or dripping (fat left over from the Sunday roast) which we had to take with us washed down with a drink of water.

We got half an hour for lunch break and had to stay outside till it was over. There was the front and back playgrounds. The boys usually played football in the back one and the girls played in the front one. We did skipping and ball games such as "Alaba Alaba", hopscotch, tig, rounders and Blind Man's Buff. Being wartime things were very scarce.

The quality of our writing materials was very poor. The pencils were plain wood called utility pencils. The paper in the jotters was very poor. When you used a rubber the paper tore! There were maps on the school walls. We were not allowed to talk in class and to look at or copy from someone else was considered a serious misconduct. The offending pupil was slapped with a cane.

I think both the teachers were very smart as they had to teach all subjects and we were well taught. Mrs. McColgan was very particular about good manners and how you spoke. You had to say "yes please" and "thank you" where it was appropriate. The priest used to visit regularly and when he came into the room we had to stand up and greet him by "Good morning" or "Good afternoon, Father" according to the time of day. The Catholics did their religious education every day after school so we Protestants got out at three o'clock and they had to stay half an hour longer. The priest came to prepare the pupils for the sacraments.

I remember too, before we got our summer holidays, we used to have a visit from the "funny man" as he was called. He was a conjurer and would bring rabbits and doves out of a hat, and do some other tricks. This was fun for us children back then as it was the only entertainment we had.

Mrs. McColgan taught the senior girls how to cook. The kitchen was just basic with a big wooden table to work on and big stove or range to cook on. There was no fancy cupboards like today. As far as I remember there were shelves to store all the equipment. We had no running water either; there was a pump at the back of the school where we got the water.

By the time I was twelve years old I had got as far as I could education-wise. You left school at fourteen then. Most of the girls went into the factories or as housemaids to the farmers and business people in the city and I suppose the boys went into labouring or farming work. I just don't know. Those who wanted a different vocation left at 12 years old and went to one of the city schools.

I left at twelve years and went into First Derry School where I finished doing commercial work as I wanted to do some kind of office work. That was 1946. The qualifying exams, or 11 plus as it later became, had just come that year but I was just that bit too old. I was twelve that April. Mrs. McColgan did her best by writing to the High School and the Education Authorities to see if I would be allowed to sit the exam but it was of no use. She thought I should have got a chance of the higher education. My younger sister, Mary, was eleven the following June 1947 so she was able to sit for it. She and a fellow pupil, Paddy King, both did it that year and passed. Mrs. McColgan was very pleased to have two pupils pass that year. I had two other sisters and two brothers who also attended Rossnagalliagh till they left at eleven and went for further education elsewhere. The names of the other members of the family who attended were Helen, Richard, Frankie and Florence.

Just about the end of the war the schools were given milk for the pupils - a third of a pint each. We got it during our eleven o'clock break. The winters were very cold then and we were always sure of snow. During the winter the milk used to freeze. There was a fireplace in both rooms, where the teachers sat, so the milk crates were put beside them until the ice melted. We used to enjoy getting around the teacher for reading as we got heated from the fire. In the wintertime the school was very cold as it had no heating so we kept our coats on.

Photo taken c1949
Front Row l to r: James King, George McLauglin, Patrick Gillespie
Second Row l to r: Annie Gillespie, Ashley Gillespie, Anthony King, Bridie Gillespie, Bertie Crossan,
Kathleen Crumley, Frankie McCracken, Iris Robinson, Tommy Logan, Mary King, Lily McLaughlin,
Vina Robinson, Fanny Campbell
Third row l to r: Lily Toland, Isobel Campbell, Mary McCracken, Helen McCracken, Sadie Gillespie,
Bertie Boyd, Charlie Gillespie, George Logan, Susan Crumley, Maria Rutherford,
Fourth Row l to r: Minnie Logan, Shelia Gillespie, Noeleen Crossan, Margaret Gillespie,
Angela Gillespie, (twins) Sammy Campbell, Joyce Robinson, Helen McLaughlin,
Coleen McEleny, Danny Toland
Fifth Row: Annie Campbell, Bridget Gillespie, William Gillespie, Danny Gillespie,
Willie Gillespie, Willie McCorkell, Joe King, William Brown, Bobby Logan, John Campbell,
Sixth row l to r: Paddy King, Rosemary Cassidy, Cissie Logan, Celine Cullinan, Doreen Gillespie,
Richard McCracken, David Boyd, Bertie Cunningham, Seamus Gillespie

Another thing is the toilets were outside at the back-end of the back playground. It wasn't very pleasant if you had to use them on a pouring wet day or in the snow. They were dry toilets that had to be emptied by the caretaker. You were not able to wash your hands either as there was no water. The caretakers may have been Mrs. W Gillespie and Mrs. Brown, parents of the pupils. I enjoyed my days at Rossnagalliagh School.

Personal Recollections

George McLaughlin attended the school from 1945-52. He gave considerable help with names of pupils and their addresses from 1950's as the rolls from this period are missing. George lived at Dam Row, Newbuildings and attended school with his sisters. They walked to school, which took about 15 minutes. In summer he wore light clothing, a shirt and short trousers and in winter jumpers, short trousers and heavy boots. The teachers at this time were Miss Reid and Mrs. McColgan. The subjects he recalls doing included arithmetic, geography, English, poetry and grammar. On the walls of the classroom were a variety of maps-countries of the world, Ireland and its provinces.

There was no specific sports day, but the children organised themselves in games and ran races around the school. George remembered clergy, inspectors, a nurse, past–pupils,the dentist and the memory man, Bobby Nichol, coming to visit the school.

Lily Bradley, George McLaughlin's sister, attended from 1944 -55. She gave a list of fellow pupils.

Lily wore a gabardine coat, boots, woollen jumpers in winter and lighter clothes in summer. Most children did not have particular clothes for school and Lily described what she wore as "ordinary ones".

Lily's teachers were Mrs. McColgan and Mrs. Foley. Inside the school were two big rooms, a corridor and an old kitchen with stairs leading to another big room at the top of the stairs. There was a place called "the black hole". In the lower room there was a little open fireplace and a small stove in the upper room.

Outside there was a wall all the way round the playground, a row of toilets and a bicycle shed. Lily took a lunch, usually just scone bread or white bread, butter or jam. This was eaten in the playground.

The visitors to the school included the nurse, Monsignor O'Doherty and other priests and clergy.

Lily also recalled Bobby Nicholl visits. She explained that he was known as " the memory man" as he could tell what day of the week you were born if given the date.

The caretaker at this time was called Joe King.
Lily recalled that the school ended at 3.30pm.

Danny Toland attended school from 1944.
Danny walked approximately half a mile to school. He wore jumpers, short trousers and most times did not have any shoes.

Danny recalled some mornings the classroom had to be swept and wood gathered for the fire before lessons began. A wood burning open fire heated the classroom. The teachers were Miss Reid and Mrs McColgan. Danny remembered being taught the 3 "R"'s and religion. They mostly studied the gospels. Visitors to the school included the priest and dentist. Danny went home at lunch time and ate bread and jam and afterwards played in the school yard. He recalled that Mrs. McColgan carried him into school one day after he had cut his feet on some broken glass. At that time she would have been near retirement age. Mrs. McColgan did not allow pupils to use bad language. One day a lad swore and was smacked and told "I am not having this Americanised filth in this school." He thought the school building was "run down". Danny left school at fourteen to help support the family as he had no father at home. (Danny's father had been killed in an accident in England where he had found work.)

Mrs Lily Keane (née Toland) now living in Cork attended from 1942.
Lily walked to school. The school building had stone walls and the classrooms were painted. Heating was supplied from a cast iron stove. She recalled having milk at break time and playing in the school yard. No school dinners were supplied and, like many of the other children, Lily ate bread and jam at break-time.

On the walls of the classroom were pictures with wooden slats (pieces of wood attached to the bottom of pictures and maps to ensure they did not roll up). Subjects taught included arithmetic, English and RE. Lily wore a gym slip and blouse. The family could not always afford new clothes.

CHAPTER 8

DRAMATIC CHANGES

One of the most dramatic changes in the life of the school took place in 1955 when a new state school was opened in Newbuildings village with an initial enrolment of about 40 pupils. This brought to an end over a century of integrated primary schooling in the Newbuildings area, and the chance for all the children in the area to intermingle. Past pupils recall that those who had gone to Rossnagalliagh, and been educated together, remained friends and meetings arranged by the author of this history can verify this. One commentated that he believed that those who attended the school during this period had not been involved in "the troubles".

After 1955 the number of children remaining at Rossnagalliagh declined. For example 37 pupils were present when Mr J L Donaghy, attendance officer, visited on 1st July 1958. In 1963 there were 39 pupils, 1964 - 44 pupils, 1965- 48 pupils, 1966-49 pupils, 1967 52 pupils, 1968-55 pupils and 1969-53 pupils.

Change in Staff and Curriculum

The retirement of Mrs. McColgan in 1957 was to bring an end to another important part of the life of the school; by this date there had been nearly a century of leadership by Mrs McColgan and her mother.

Mrs. McColgan and Mrs Elliott had been an important influence on the lives of many children over a wide catchment area. Personal contact with parents and families by the two Principals was reflected in the decision by parents of all religions to send their children to Rossnagalliagh, rather than other schools closer at hand.

Miss Margaret McEllroy (later Mrs McGinnis) was to replace Mrs McColgan as Principal and she was assisted by Noeleen McColgan and Noeleen Naylor. Although there were children leaving Rossnagalliagh to attend Grammar schools after completing the 11+ from 1947, the majority were supposed to move to Intermediate or "Technical" Secondary Schools. However, it took time to implement the 1947 Education Act. By the end of 1950 – 51 there were only 10 county and 2 voluntary secondary schools in Northern Ireland. Many children, therefore, were to remain at primary school until leaving to go to work at 14 years old.

Retirement of Mrs McColgan c 1957
Back row l to r: Nan Cassidy, Peggy McIlroy (Principal), Noeleen McColgan (daughter of Mrs McColgan), Dora Gillespie, Annie Gillespie, Jeannie McCorkell, Mrs Orr, Mrs McCracken, Mrs Walker, Front row l to r: Rev Keilt, Matt Stewart, Tom McColgan (Mrs McColgan's husband), Monsignor O'Doherty, Mrs McColgan, ? , Rev Brennan

By 1957, the school leaving age had risen to 15 and the rolls for 1965 show that pupils in Rossnagalliagh continued to attend until they reached Primary 9, although only five are shown due to the very low numbers attending at this period. For example, Martin Kelly is found on the rolls for September 1965 at the age of 14 years and 10 months old and Margaret Cassidy was 14 years and 8 months old in 1964. The first written evidence of pupils moving to a secondary school is found in the 1969 roll, as the rolls for the 1950's are missing. Out of the seven children in Primary Seven in that year, Sean Flanaghan, Steven Bulford and Jeremiah Kelly went to St Columb's College and Kevin Foley, Claire McNamee, Anne Toland and Bernadette Brennan went to to St Brecan's Secondary School.

In 1956 a new programme was introduced by the Ministry of Education (A Programme for Primary Schools)[1] which emphasised age, ability and aptitude. This replaced year to year schemes in different subjects. Craft work was again promoted and boys were instructed how to make raffia mats or rugs but this took second place to subjects such as arithmetic, geography, English, composition or poetry, nature study, needlework, Hygiene and PE. However Cookery was not on the syllabus as the kitchen was to be used to prepare school dinners after 1955. Past pupils are unsure if history was part of the curriculum but, interestingly, school projects involving firms outside the country seem to be included in the early 1960's, which encouraged pupils to actively participate in a wider based curriculum.

c 1954/5 Back row l to r: Margaret Cassidy, Gerry Kelly, Paddy Phillips, John King, Marie Gillespie
Front row l to r: Sadie Browne, Eileen Mclaughlin, Gerard Gillespie, John Brown,
George (Ordy) Phillips, May Phillips

Background of Pupils

The addresses of pupils at the school in the 1950's and into the 1960's narrowed to within a very short distance of the school compared to any period from the beginning of the school's history. They came mostly from a new social housing estate in Newbuildings called Foyle Crescent , some of whom had lived in Dam Row , a small number came from Dunhugh-Half Mile Hill (later known as Woodside Road), Rossnagalliagh, Prehen, Kittybane, and one family came from Cullion, Co Tyrone for a short period. In the early 1960's another row of houses was built in Newbuildings called Ballyorr Drive. Most children during this period walked to school, although some came by bus (see Margaret Boyd's account).

There is no record of father's occupations in this period although local sources indicate that a minority of pupils continued to come from farming families, such as O'Kane's of Rossnagalliagh or Flanagan's of Dunhugh.

However as the number of farms under tillage declined after the war and farmers began to own labour-saving tractors, it is probable few fathers were employed as labourers, and therefore unemployment in the area was to rise substantially. Fishing on the Foyle for a few months, therefore, continued to provide much needed work in the area, and at least one father is known to have worked on construction sites in England. The movement of fathers as agricultural and construction workers to Britain was probably a constant factor throughout the history of the school, although there is no written evidence available.

Local firms, especially the shirt industry, were to be in decline by 1960's which had mostly employed women and therefore was not offset by an influx of outside firms such as Du Pont, which set up in 1960 at Maydown.

School Dinners
School meals were to be available at Rossngalliagh for the first time from 1955, although some pupils continued to bring a lunch from home. The dinners were prepared in the newly built Primary school in Newbuildings by Mrs. McClintock and Mrs. Ellen McGarrigle, and served in Rossnagalliagh by Mrs Sadie Hamilton from "the White Houses" in Magheramason. She was helped by the older girls who also helped to clean the former class room now used as a canteen and washed the dishes. Mrs. Hamilton was replaced by Mrs. Cissie Saint, Mrs. Nora Ferry and Mrs. Susan Foley who continued to work in the small kitchen at the back of the building until the school closed. Milk continued to be available during a break in the morning at around 11 o'clock.

Keeping the School Clean
By 1959 there does not seem to be a caretaker available to give an overall clean during the summer break. Mrs. W. Gillespie of Newbuildings Street, who had been caretaker in the 1930's and 40's, therefore,was contacted by the Principal, Miss Margaret McElroy, by letter. She outlined the cleaning she felt was necessary, and asked Mrs Gillespie to arrange for someone to do it.

The Principal instructed that the floors were to be scrubbed in the two classrooms and the two porches. Paintwork was to be washed in both rooms, on the wooden panels and doors. Miss McElroy advised if "Flash" was used, not too much was to be put in the water as "it lifts the paint", windows were also to be cleaned as the Principal liked the school "to be nice".

Mrs. Gillespie was also asked to "get one of the boys to give the toilets a good scrubbing too as they get untidy with so many children using them". Although we have no record of which boy Mrs Gillespie got to respond to the request the letter clearly shows that the Principal thought it was a task one of her male pupils should undertake.

William Gillespie (not a relation of the caretaker) however, recalled the toilet facilities in this period were mostly used by girls, while boys used a drain or guttering running along the ground into a near-by field. This probably would not have been with the teacher's knowledge.

Children's Health.
Pupils in the 1950's and 1960's continued to have a nurse calling at the school to examine the children's hair for lice, sound their chest, looking at ears, eyes and throat and to check their height and weight. A doctor also attended to administer injections for polio which was on the increase, while tuberculosis was on the wane due to a B.C.G. injection. William Gillespie and Margaret Boyd also remembered a dentist visiting the school. He used a parked caravan and William recalled a young girl emerging with blood pouring from her mouth!

The letter discussed above was thanks to Mrs Annie McLaughlin- a past pupil

Personal Accounts

Mrs Mary Devine (née King) lived at Rossnagalliagh. Mary wrote the following piece about her schooldays , 1946-55

Rossnagalliagh School was not a big building. There were two classrooms, a kitchen and two attic rooms. In the early days of the school the kitchen and upstairs rooms served as living quarters for the teacher and her family. Like my mother before me I went to the school when I was aged five. I remember drawing on a black slate with chalk. We learned to count on an abacus of wooden beads and there were wooden blocks to play with.

My teacher was Mrs. Foley. She lived in Spencer Road in the Waterside. The other teacher was Mrs. McColgan. She lived at Upper Burndennett. They (the teacher and her children) came to school by bus.

I lived just five minutes walk from school. Most pupils came from the village of Newbuildings and surrounding district and for some that meant a long walk. Everyone brought a packed lunch as meals were not provided. Free milk was delivered every day and everyone got a small bottle each. Lunch was eaten outside on dry days and in the classrooms on wet days. Lunch was just bread and jam or margarine (not butter).

The school had a good playground space. The older boys played football at the back of the school. Girls played a variety of games such as skipping, jumping, hopscotch and different ball games.

The outside walls (of the school building) were built with grey stone and two doors led into each classroom.The classroom furniture consisted of the teachers table and chair and rows of desks and a few cupboards for storing books. There was a large blackboard hanging on one wall. The teacher would have used that a lot when teaching us sums and spellings. On the other walls hung maps- a long map of the world and a map of Ireland. These maps helped us a lot when we had geography class. The rooms were heated with an open fire in the "lower room" and a small black stove in the "upper room". My father was caretaker for the school and sometimes my brothers and I would have to light the fires early before the teachers arrived - a job we hated doing. The coal for the fires was delivered by the shop owner in the village.

We learned a lot at primary school. We did reading, writing, spelling, arithmetic, geography and our times tables. We were made to practice our tables until we knew them off by heart.

We also learned poetry and did a little drama. Girls were taught basic cookery and we learned how to knit and sew. We started knitting simple things like scarves and hand mittens. Then we were taught how to knit socks. We were taught how to turn the heel and close the toe.

I think we were well taught as I remember a lot from school days. I suppose that is because we learned a lot off by heart. It was a small school but a happy school when I was there. There were about sixty pupils attending. Our last day in primary school was on our fourteenth birthday. Then it was off to find work and earn a living.

Charlotte Temple (née McLaughlin) attended the school from 1948-58.
Charlotte lived at the Dam Row and walked to school. She thought the school looked much as it does today (it is now a family home), but obviously not as modern. Charlotte wore her sisters' "castoffs" mostly. Her teachers were Mrs. Mary McColgan and Miss Peggy McElroy from Strabane, (although the teacher seemed to be called Peggy her proper name was Margaret). The subjects Charlotte recalled doing at Rossnagalliagh included maths, english, geography, religion, knitting, sewing, art and music. On the walls of the school room the teacher sometimes put up the children's art- work.

Charlotte ate a lunch provided by her mother, but dinner was supplied in later years. This was eaten at one end of the classroom, near the cloakroom. There was a small room at the back of the school referred to as "the kitchen". This was used to serve out dinner which was delivered by container van. Pupils often helped to wash up dishes and tidy classrooms and the kitchen after dinner. After dinner-time she played in the playground which she remembered as a "small area".

Mrs Shelia McCallion (née Gillespie) attended the school from 1948-52.
Shelia lived at Magheracannon, Kittybane Road and walked to school which was about 2-3miles. She wore clothes made by her mother, kilts, petticoats, knitted jumpers, cardigans, pixies, scarves, and gloves. She also wore "good" coats, shoes and socks which the family could afford as her father had a good wage

as a warder/male nurse in a mental hospital in Londonderry. Her teachers were Mrs. Foley and Mrs. McColgan. Shelia recalled doing arithmetic and poetry-she remembered learning an action poem particularly. However she did not recall doing any examinations. Unfortunately Shelia was slapped for writing with her left hand but happier memories are of her getting a photograph taken in the playground.

In 1952 Shelia attended first confession which was held in the kitchen of the school. As the number of pupils was low at this time only five Catholic children learnt the catechism around the teacher's desk while the Protestant children were out in the playground. The family then moved to live in a new estate in Creggan, Londonderry and Shelia went to Long Tower Primary School.

Mrs Kathleen Donaghey (née Crumley) was a pupil from 1949 -59. Her sister, Susan Foley, kindly passed on the information and gave the names of three fellow pupils, Sean Ferry, John Donnell and Sarah Brown. Kathleen's teachers were Mrs. Foley, Mrs. McColgan and Miss McElroy. School holidays included a week at Christmas and Easter, 4 weeks in the summer and 2 weeks in October (potato gathering holidays). She walked to school from Dunhugh and wore "everyday" clothes. She was accompanied by Charlotte McLaughlin and Ashley Gillespie from Newbuildings Street (now Victoria Road). Also in her class were Thomas Gillespie, Bobbie Holmes, Anthony King, Peter Cassidy, Mabel McClelland, Evelyn McClelland, Margaret Brown and Doris Arthur.

Mrs Evelyn Campbell (née McClelland) attended from 1952-55 and had come from Groarty School. She recalled the classrooms were both downstairs on either side of the doorway and that the pupils thought the upstairs was haunted! Evelyn remembered being taught to do embroidery and made a tray cloth. She particularly did not like geography, but thought they did not do history.

Evelyn left Rossnagalliagh when the new Primary School opened in Newbuildings in 1955. She was aged 11. Evelyn was to go to work when she was 15.

Ms Sadie Browne attended the school from1954 - 63 and **Margaret Boyd (nee Cassidy)** from 1954 – 1969. Sadie had previously attended Waterside School. Sadie and Margaret lived in Foyle Crescent and walked to school. Sometimes Margaret took a bus which cost 1d. Sadie's brothers John, and Gerry and sisters Kathleen and

Margaret also attended Rossnagalliagh. The back of the school was white washed and gravel had been spread all around the school where the children played. The windows were covered in mesh to prevent them from being broken. Margaret wore knitted jumpers, kilts or pleated skirts, fur boots, tights and a gabardine coat in winter. In summer she wore dresses and skirts. Most of the clothes were shop bought. Her mother was very particular about her children's' appearance. Margaret thought she was very "fussy". Each September Margaret wore new clothes and shoes to school. Her hair was put in ringlets. She carried her school books in a leather school bag and had a wooden pencil case.

c 1958/9 Back row l to r: Miss Peggy McIlroy, Marie Gillespie, Margaret McDaid, May Phillips, Sadie Browne, Bridie Gillespie, Eileen McLaughlin, Veronica McDaid, Mary McNamee, Margaret Cassidy, Miss Noeleen McColgan
Second row l to r: John Ferry, Ann Kelly, Danny Ferry, Eddie Phillips, Danny Brown, Deidre McNamee, Martin Kelly, Michael Kelly, Terence McNamee, Brendan (Benny) Kelly,
Front Row l to r: Angus Gillespie, James Gillespie, Francis (Francie) Cassidy, Patrick (Paddy) Phillips, John King, Gerry Brown

Miss Noeleen McColgan left Rossnagalliagh in 1964. Older girls, such as Margaret, assisted the teachers for short periods in the classroom if the teacher was late, or had to leave school for any reason. The following subjects were on the syllabus- arithmetic geography, nature study, English-composition, poetry, grammar, needlework, PE and singing. The children also learnt about hygiene. On the walls of the classroom were maps, and there was a globe of the world which was used in geography lessons. The pupils were encouraged to write to companies enquiring about a range of products, such as Cadbury's chocolate or to Australian companies about Merino wool, as part of class projects. At Christmas time the children may have taken part in a school play or sang in a school choir at church. On a warm day the children read outside, which was well received as it was an escape from the classroom. There was no day set aside as a "sports day" but during PE Margaret recalled using hoola hoops, bean bags and skipping ropes. The children also played rounders.

School dinners were available in this period. Margaret and Sadie served dinners and helped to clean up after the younger pupils. The dinner ladies were called Mrs. Cissie Saint, Mrs. Nora Ferry and Mrs. Susan Foley. The dinners were brought from the new Primary School at Newbuildings, where they had been made by Mrs. McClintock and Mrs. Ellen McGarrigle. Small bottles of milk were available at break time in the morning. The milk was placed near the fire in winter to melt the ice on top and this produced an unpleasant taste.

There was a caretaker, but Margaret could not recall who it was. Visitors to the school included the clergy. Monsignor O'Doherty brought sweets for the pupils and at the end of term gave each child a painting book. Margaret believed the School Inspector was also a frequent caller as this was the Principal's first post. Miss McElroy was in her twenties. The Inspector also regularly accessed the number of pupils at the school as the numbers were very low.

A doctor and nurse took care of the general health of the pupils. They measured height and weight, sounded the chest, examined ears and throat and examined the children for hair lice. The doctor gave injections against polio. Margaret remembered that one boy ran away from the doctor as he was afraid of getting an injection but the teacher caught him and brought him back. A school dentist also called and used a mobile caravan as a surgery.

The teacher kept a cane, although Margaret does not recall being punished. However she remembered trying to hide the cane behind the school clock which fell down and broke!

Margaret also recalled that she and Sadie had chased a boy around the school but the boy took a mop out of the store cupboard and put mud on it and began to chase the girls. When he stopped to put water on the mop the girls locked him in the store and returned to class. When the teacher asked where the boy was she was told "in the store"   The teacher then opened the door of the store but the boy thought it was the girls returning and hit out at the teacher with the mop dirtying her clothes in the process.   He was sent home and had to write a letter of apology to the teacher. The girls did not own up!!

Margaret left school at 15 years of age and went to work in Woolworths. Miss McElroy gave her a leather purse and rosary beads before she left the school. Later in life Margaret returned to education and taught locally.

She considered the education the pupils received at Rossnagalliagh ensured all could read, write and count well, due largely to Miss McElroy's teaching. Margaret thought Miss McElroy was a kind teacher who encouraged confidence in her pupils by telling them they could do anything they wanted. She thought the pupils who had attended during her time at school turned out well. They were good citizens and had a good community spirit.

Bridgeen Rutherford (née O'Kane) attended the school from 1964-1969 and then attended Strabane Convent Primary School. She wrote the following account.

We lived next door to Rossnagalliagh School so did not have far to travel- across the field in fact. We were always early for school except I distinctly remember the day the School Inspector was due to visit. We were all warned the previous day by the Principal to be on time. But unfortunately we slept in and I remember not wanting to go to school to be told off. We came to school with our heads down and I distinctly remember hanging my coat up in the cloakroom and not wanting to come out as the teacher was extremely annoyed.

When I was a small child I remember one of the older pupils would come up to bring us down to school. It was not always possible to go across the field and the alternative was the busy main road to Strabane. On a recent conversation with the girl who collected me and took me home we realised that she was in fact only a couple of years older than me at that time!

We went home for our lunch/dinner every day as in a farm house dinner was always ready at 12.15pm – 12.30pm. When dinner was finished at Rossnagalliagh School one of the older pupils in the school was sent up with scraps from the school dinners to be fed to our pigs; well fed pigs! We knew then it was time to go back for afternoon classes. The only time we were allowed school dinners was when it was one of our birthdays.

I remember learning our time tables. They were only a couple of us in our class. We were made to line up along the window and asked our tables in turn. If we did not know them we got a slap on the hand by the principal with the T square. This normally was hung on the wall near the stove. Sometimes I would just want to jump out of the window and run home across the field to a safe haven.

c1968/9 l to r: Andrew Watts, Martin Burke, Michael O'Doherty, Kathleen Brennan, Bridgeen O'Kane, Ann Foley, Michael Flanagan, Steven Bulford

CHAPTER 9

THE CLOSING YEARS

In the 1970's the number of children at the school was to increase substantially principally due to a new housing estate in Newbuildings called Primity Crescent and Primity Terrace, and a number also came from Prehen. Children in smaller numbers also came from Foyle Crescent,Ballyorr Drive, Dunhugh, Rossnagalliagh and Half Mile Hill (now called Woodside Road).

Photo taken at St Columba's School c 1977 showing last pupils
who had attended Rossnaglliagh before its closure.
Back row l to r: Patrick King, John McBride, Emma McLaughlin, Jude O'Donnell, Stephen Latimer,
Martin Devine, Darren McNeill, Seamus Flanagan, Michael Gallagher
Second Row l to r: Patrick Gillespie, Damien Doherty, Paul McLaughlin, Aibhne O'Kane,
Sinead Simpson, Mary McGonagle, Rory McNamee, Terry Geddis, Adrian Kerr
Front l to r: Margaret Gillespie, Sinead Robb, Tara Hegarty, Bronagh Hegarty, Anne Marie Ferry,
Linda Sharkey, Tracey Cooke, Sheena Robb, Donna Smith, Teacher Paddy Flanagan
(past pupil of Rossnagalliagh)

There were 74 pupils in 1970, 153 pupils in 1971, 89 pupils in 1972, 108 pupils in 1973, 102 pupils in 1974, 129 pupils in 1975 and 128 pupils in 1976. Interestingly the numbers of pupils attending in the closing years of the school were around the same number attending Rossnagalliagh when Paddy Browne was as a pupil in 1905, when they had to squeeze into one classroom.

The fabric of the school and outbuildings, generally, was deteriorating and as plans for a new school were in the pipeline, no further work was undertaken at this time. Instead three mobile classrooms were added in a nearby field belonging to John O'Kane for a nominal fee. Rosemary Campbell, who attended from 1966 to 1977, (niece of a former teacher) remembered space in the original classroom was also restricted as books were stored in Hunter and Palmers biscuit tins.

Unlike the majority of pupils up to this decade only one family is recorded to have walked to school in 1970's, as most were to come by bus or car. The road to school had become increasingly busy from 1950's, due to the closure of the railways which caused an increase in lorries, and there were no footpaths provided to ensure the children's safety. The heavy traffic also affected the comings and goings on sports day as children crossed the road to a field opposite the school provided for the purpose in front of John Roulston's house. Apart from celebrating the end of WWII, this seems to be the only period when a sports day was included in the school year.

Staff and Curriculum

The Principal, Mrs. McGinnis, taught the senior pupils until she retired in 1973. She was replaced by Mr. David O'Donnell, who was to be the last Principal, from 1973-77. He was also to be the first man to teach at Rossnagalliagh, unlike other schools in the area such as Bready or Killymallaght, which had had male principals from their inception.

Miss Geraldine Kelly, from Draperstown, joined the staff in 1972 as did Mrs. Anne Fitzpatrick. Anne left the staff for a period of two years to gain further teacher training as new legislation had been introduced for primary teachers. She was to return from 1975-77. A Miss Doherty and a Miss McCaville taught along with Mrs. Vera Harte in the last days of the school. All teachers by this period had attended teacher - training colleges in Belfast.

*Photo taken at St Columba's School showing last pupils at Rossnagalliagh and includes
Mrs Vera Harte who taught at Rossnagalliagh for a short period.
Back Row l to r: Mark Sheerin, Bridget Geaghty, Sinead Simpson, Paula McGee,
Ursula Kennelly, Tracey Pulis
Second Row l to r: Caroline Sharkey, Joanne Smith, Fiona Kell, Elizabeth Mohammat,
Sheena Robb, Mary McMonagle, Damien Doherty, Michael Gallagher
Front Row l to r: Donna Smith, Tracey Cooke, Paul McLaughlin, Adrian Kerr, Patrick Gillespie
Patrick F Gillespie, Matthew Callan, Aoibhe O'Kane, Gerard Clancy*

There is no evidence that the curriculum in this decade was to differ significantly from that of 1956 Programme for Primary Schools, with English and Mathematics predominant, as considerable pressure continued to attain literacy and numeracy by Primary seven.[1]

However, in the 1974 Teachers Guide, a new course called Environmental Studies was introduced which included the teaching of History. While the new course was not always implemented in Primary schools, there is evidence that some attempt at a local history project was introduced at Rossnagalliagh in the 1970's, as witnessed in the interview of past pupil, Paddy Brown.

This might have been due less to the slow decrease in central planning and more to the interests of teaching staff and time allocation.[2]

All the children were to leave school by the age of 11 in the 1970's to attend a secondary school. Although the 11+ examination had been in place for nearly 30 years it is interesting to read Siobhan Kennelly's account where she recalls not having to undertake the examination to gain a grammar school place in 1977.

Mr O'Donnell confirmed that for one year only the examination was not to take place, instead the principal of a school was to assess the children. However, he believed that this resulted in too many children being assessed for grammar school places and the examination reappeared, in different forms, over the following years.

The school closed in 1977, and although most schools built and supported by the Irish Society reverted back to them at this stage, a controversy over ownership between the Irish Society and the Catholic Church began. It ended with the Irish Society eventually passing ownership to the Church in writing. The school was then sold and became a private house in the 1980's.[3]

1   Circular A/35/B/8/C/9 of 1956 , Ministry of Education Belfast 26th June 1956 Also reports of primary School Programme Committee Belfast HMSO1956

2   Northern Ireland Teacher's guide Belfast 1974 History Teaching in P7 p 101

3   Curl, The Honourable and the Irish Society, p361, the transcript of the Disagreement taken from report by Vivienne Aldous, Society archivist 2002

Personal Accounts

Siobhan Kennelly (now living in Sydney, Australia) attended Rossnagalliagh from 1971-1977. She wrote the following account of her time at school and also gave an interview.

Siobhan attended Rossnagalliagh Primary School from September 1971 when she turned 5, until June 1977. She recalled moving to P3 after P1, but having to repeat P7 after moving to St Columba's School in 1977. The children's clothes in 1970's did not differ much from those worn in 1950's as Siobhan wore skirts or kilts, cardigans, long socks, boots in winter and an anorak. She carried a case for her books. She walked from her home in Primity Terrace to Villa's public house where she got a bus to school. As more care was taken of the children's safety by this time the children were helped off the bus by the teaching staff. Teachers also ensured the pupils safely crossed the busy road at the end of the school day to get a bus home. While waiting for the bus boys gathered chestnuts and played a game of "conkers".

The outside of the school building had rough plaster which was painted white with a blue trim. The walls of the school room were covered with pupils' work including a chart which indicated the name of the pupil and the books the children had read. Siobhan was an enthusiastic reader. The curriculum at this period included maths, Religious Instruction (New Testament) comprehension, poetry, reading, tables, and PE. There was an annual sports day usually held across the road in a field. One year it was in a field owned by Mr O'Kane. Children continued to learn their tables and ABC by rote. An abacus, as shown below, was used in Infant classes.

photo shows an abacus which was used to help children count.

Siobhan's account

Rossnagalliagh closed at the end of the school year in 1977 and re-opened in its new premises in Newbuildings as St Columba's Primary School in September 1977. I spent my final year of primary school at St Columba's and went to Thornhill College in 1978. I was one of the lucky few who managed to avoid the 11plus exam and was simply assessed by Master O'Donnell to be fit for grammar school. Thanks for that, David!

I have many memories of Rossnagalliagh and think of it fondly as I drive past on my visits home. In no particular order- here are my memories!

Worn flagstones in the entrance.

I remember Mrs Ferry in the kitchen and the smell of fish and white sauce in the dining room. Irish dancing with Mary McLaughlin in the same dining room, converted to a dance studio after school had finished for the day, and wishing it was over!

It was a treat to be picked to go and collect the milk for the class- a crate of milk- often warm in the sunshine- and sticking the little straws through the foil caps. It was an even better treat to get sent to deliver the "brock" (dinner time scraps of food) to the O'Kane's farm next door and be rewarded with crab apples.

I remember playtime in the front playground which was covered in gravel. Girls sang songs such as "jelly on a plate" while skipping using two long ropes or jumping in and out of elastic bands in a game called "German jumps". Other games included throwing jacks to indicate how many times to throw balls in the air or throwing two balls against the wall, sometimes under a leg.

Netball was part of PE and annually games were played against other schools. On one occasion we were playing netball after school and there was no net at one end for some reason- someone had to stand on a chair and hold a wastepaper bin as a makeshift net! I don't remember the details exactly but Master O'Donnell and I had a disagreement about the rules that day and it ended with him storming off midgame! He and I had many disagreements as I recall. My Mum gave up arguing with me early on-Master O'Donnell didn't! It was no surprise to anyone that I went on to become a lawyer and got paid to argue!

I remember most vividly visits from Father McConnellogue, RIP. We looked forward to his visits because he used to donate the biscuits that Mrs Ferry bought to him with his cup of tea to the first to answer his questions.

I don't remember much learning by rote in those days but I can still recite the names of the 12 apostles and the 10 commandments with ease! The thought of a Mikado biscuit was a great incentive to learn! It wasn't until I went to Thornhill and learnt some Irish that I worked out that Father McConnellogue was not addressing Master O'Donnell as an "oyster" but rather "an Mhiastir" - I often puzzled over that!

Making my Holy Communion with all the teachers at the back of the little chapel exclaiming as each of us arrived is a clear memory, as was the great occasion when Brian Ferry RIP and myself got picked to present the newly ordained Bishop Daly with a glass fronted bookcase from the parish.

I remember the warmth of the portable classrooms with the gas heaters and the windows fogging up on cold and wet days and working my way along the portables parked in the fields until finally making it into Master O'Donnells' class in the schoolroom of the main building. The toilets were still outdoors though and a most unpleasant place to visit on a winter's day.

I remember Ann McCauley, Clare Ward, Teresa Devine and Elaine Frazer as my classmates and Mrs Hart and Miss Kelly as some of my teachers.

I loved my time at Rossnagalliagh. For me St Columba's was not the same- it had none of the charm of the old schoolhouse and my memories of primary school are most firmly of Rossnagalliagh. I had a great time there and received an excellent education-for that I am most grateful!

*One of the final photographs
to be taken at Rossnagalliagh
before its closure.
River Foyle in background
Back row l to r: Deidre O'Flanaghan,
Margaret Flanagan, Caroline
McCloskey, Nuala McDaid
Second row l to r Helen Arnett, Patricia
Phillips, Florence O'Brien, Maureen Ferry,
Maresa Gormley
Front Row l to r Eugene Arnett,
Michael Dunne, Robert McDaid*

Miss Geraldine Kelly came from Draperstown. She taught in Rossnagalliagh from 1972 until its closure in 1977.

Geraldine recalled that the school was opened in the morning and the fires were lit before the staff and children arrived.

The main classroom was on the left of the entrance and on the right was the lunch room. Due to the increase in the number of pupils mobile classrooms were placed in a field belonging to Mr O'Kane, a neighbouring farmer; a laneway joined the school property and these classrooms.

The curriculum included the 11+ examination and the school gained good results. Lunch was available in the middle of the day and was prepared in the old kitchen at the back of the school. This room was liable to flooding but the dinner ladies, Mrs Saint and Mrs Ferry worked on, wearing wellingtons if necessary.

The toilets for staff and pupils were separate from the school and Geraldine remembered it was necessary to take an umbrella if the weather was wet. However, the roof in the toilet block leaked so it may not have been much drier there. Generally the school buildings were in need of major work but Geraldine stated that as a new school was to be built in the area, monies were not being put into Rossnagalliagh. The visitors to the school between1972-77 included the Catholic clergy from St Columb's, Waterside, and school inspectors –a Miss Bennet may have been the Inspector in 1975. She was preceded by a male District Inspector, whose name Geraldine could not recall.

The Irish Society continued to be involved with the school and gave grants for new equipment. Representatives came annually to the school in the springtime and Geraldine remembered their arrival. The children were on their best behaviour.
Geraldine moved to the new St Columba's School when it opened in 1977. The children walked from Rossnagalliagh to the new building. Parents of the pupils moved equipment and books by van and car.

Mr David O'Donnell Principal from January 1973 to June 1977 wrote the following piece which gives a real insight into the school building which had not changed to any extent in over a century.

Fr. Stephen Kearney, curate of Glendermott Parish, handed me the keys of Rossnagalliagh on the 1st January 1973. The keys consisted of a very large brown coloured key and three normal sized shiny keys. When I arrived at the school it looked more like a barricaded old house than a primary school. I found out that the large key opened the front door of the old building.

The front door was made from heavy wood and had a black steel latch which was used to open it. I thought that maybe it was the original door of the school. When I opened the door I found myself in a very small entrance hall which opened up into three different rooms.

The floor of the hall was tiled with rough stone tiles which were uneven. The floors of the two large rooms, one a classroom and the other a dining hall, were bare wooden floors which were bleached at intervals to keep them clean.

The left hand door opened up into a classroom which was quite small. I had to put my desk tight to the wall and when sitting at the desk would have my back to the class. Needless to say, I only sat at the table in the morning before class or in the evening when the children had gone home.

The right hand door opened into the dining hall which was bigger than the classroom. Compared to modern schools the dining hall was tiny but it seemed to be big enough to cope with the number of children who took dinners at the school. This room was also used for PTA meetings, parish committee meetings, bingo, discos, and as a general meeting place for the different social groups in this area of Glendermott Parish. These activities continued until the new school was built in 1977.

The third door went straight down into the kitchen which was about six inches lower than the rest of the school. It had a cement floor. This was a very small kitchen and was scarcely large enough to permit normal cooking activities.

Mrs. Saint was the cook and her assistant was Mrs. Nora Ferry. I don't know how they managed but the dinners were always delivered on time and of a high standard.
Once the kitchen was flooded and they still managed to cook the dinner in their wellingtons!
The Bishop of the time, Dr Edward Daly, visited the school on a particularly wet day and commented that we were the only Primary school in the diocese with a swimming pool. He also added that he was recommending that we would get a new school.

At this time the windows of the old building had grills to prevent passers-by from breaking them. The toilets of the school were outside at the back and the children and teachers had only cold water to wash their hands. I had to put a lock on the single teacher's toilet because it was no longer a school with only female teachers!
The school was surrounded by a small playground which was barely large enough to allow the children to play games. A small wall, just under 3 feet high, separated the children from the fast moving traffic on the main Strabane-Derry Road. One of our parents was involved in a serious accident outside the school when her car was in a collision with a car on the main road.

There was an attic room in the school as well, which was accessed through the kitchen door. When you entered the kitchen door you turned sharp left and up the stairs. At that time a lot of old roll book and registers were stored there. The earliest dated to the 1860's. I would guess that this attic room was used as the teacher's bedroom in this properly named school-house.

We had four classrooms in use in 1973; the old classroom in the school and the three mobile classrooms in John O'Kane's field beside the school. He leased this part of the field for a nominal fee to the parish for the school. He himself had children at the school.

There was no telephone in the school and I had to use the phone in O'Kane's house which was close to the school! John O'Kane also allowed us to use his field close to the school for the annual school sports.

The children who attended the school came from the Newbuildings and Prehen areas. Most of the children who came to the school arrived by bus except for one family from Woodside Road who sometimes walked to school up that dangerous main road. At the time we tried to get a footpath constructed from Newbuildings to the school but the idea was always turned down by the authorities. Now there is a footpath and no school. There were two gates into the school - one large gate which allowed cars to be driven into the playground and one small heavy gate for walkers.

Conclusion

Rossnagalliagh was in many ways typical of many of the rural National Schools built in the first half of the 19th Century. Its classrooms were basic with rows of desks, maps on the wall and a small fire behind the teacher's desk to heat the room.

Many of the pupils who attended came from farming or labouring families who had little extra income and attendance was affected by the need to bring in additional earnings. Ill health also affected attendance and epidemics of various kinds, particularly before the onset of the National Health Service, closed the school altogether.

Throughout its history learning by rote was part of the curriculum but the teaching staff always adjusted to new ideas and as a result the children benefitted. Past pupils considered the education they received at Rossnagalliagh to be particularly good. Ongoing problems included the lack of space within the school and in the playground, which seems never to have been overcome, although this did not interfere with the high standard of education, nor fun at break time.

Although the school was run by a Catholic manager, and included Roman Catholic religious teaching, it was not to the exclusion of the Protestant children who attended for most of its history. It may, therefore, have been one of the few primary schools to have been truly integrated for over a century providing a blueprint for those in 1980's who called for integrated education, although the latter was deliberate and structured rather than arising from local circumstances.

BIBLIOGRAPHY

PRIMARY SOURCES

Records from PRONI archives –
ED/6/3/5/1-Folio 17-Inspectors reports 1909-1935-re cookery classes, playground and classroom space. desks, retirement of Mrs. Elliot and Mrs. McColgan's move out of the school
ED/1/27 -290-317-45; Report on Application for salary for Sarah Crumley
SCH 1345/1/1, SCH 1345/1/2 and SCH 1345/1/3 –intermittent rolls from 1860 - 1950 includes details of pupils coming from other schools, addresses, father's occupations, examination details and fees.
SCH/1675; Bready School;
SCH/ 1088;Killymallaght School
SCH /1418; Greerstown School

The Honourable Irish Society records, Guildhall Library /
National Archives Kew contain:-
Irish Society Deputations Reports 1827 p 3, 12, 14, 18
CLA/049/EM/01/27; 1844. Report by Society re teacher Margaret Nauree
CLA/049/EM/01/051; 1879.Report by Society's agent about MJ Curry's call for an enlargement to the school-National Archives, Kew.
CLA/049/EM/01/052; 1880, Report by the Irish Society's agent on the proposal for a new school to be built-

Ordnance Survey Memoirs
Colby, Thomas, Col., 'Ordnance Survey of the County of Londonderry Vol 1', Dublin Hodge & Smith, 1837 and N. W. Books, Limavady 1990
Day, Angelique, Patrick McWilliams, Lisa English and Nóirin Dobson (eds) ,Ordnance Survey Memoirs of Ireland, Parishes of Londonderry XIII, 1831-8; Clondermot and the Waterside, Vol 34', The Institute of Irish Studies, Queen's University, Belfast.

Other sources
'Notes for the teachers in connection with the programme of instruction for national schools' - Office of National Education, Dublin 1913

Northern Ireland Teachers Guide, Belfast, 1974

'Report of Primary schools Programme Committee', Belfast HMSO 1956

Rolls; 1918-44 and 1923-27 and Daily Report Books which also includes number of children attending, holidays and visitors to Rossnagalliagh-private source

Fraser, Grace and Valerie Morgan, *In the Frame- Integrated Education in Northern Ireland: the implications of expansion* Centre for the Study of Conflict UU

In the Shadow of the Tail of the Fox", A History of Newbuildings & District -Newbuildings & District Archaeological & Historical Society

Secondary Sources

Aldous, Vivienne E,'*A Brief Historical Narrative of the Origins and Constitution of the Honourable the Irish Society'*, London, 1993

Bardon, Jonathan, '*A History of Ulster'*, The Blackstaff Press Ltd., 1992

Beckett, JC, '*The Making of Modern Ireland 1603-1923'* Pub1973

Curl, James Stevens, '*The Honourable The Irish Society and the Plantation of Ulster, 1608-2001'*, Philimore & Co Ltd,2000

Curl, James Stevens, '*The Londonderry Plantation 1609-1914'*, Pub., Philimore & Co Ltd 1986

Coolahan, John, '*Irish Education: its History and Structure'*, Dublin, 1981

Dowling , PJ, '*A History of Irish Education'*, 1971

Durcan, Thomas Joseph, '*History of Irish education from 1800'*, Dragon Books, 1972

Laird, Ernest Gordon, '*A Short History of Methodism in Londonderry'*,Antrim, 1996

Lyons, FSL, '*Ireland since the Famine'*, Fontana Press, 1985

Reed, Charles, '*An Historical Narrative of the Origins and Constitution of the Honourable the Irish Society'*,

Roulston Alexander, '*The Roulstons of Co Donegal, Ireland'*, Florida, 1998.

Travers, Pauric, '*Settlements & Divisions Ireland 1870-1922'*, Helicon Ltd, 1988

Turner, John, *Magheramason 1878-1978'*, Strule Press, Omagh, 1978

Newspapers and Periodicals

Familia, Vol 2 No 8 1992

The Londonderry Standard 1839

The Londonderry Journal 1880

APPENDICES

Appendix i

Who attended and where did they come from?

Below are all the available rolls, 1918- 21: 1929 - 35; 1935 - 41; 1942 - 44; 1960-77 which came from a private source. Also included is information gathered from school registers from 1860's intermittingly to 1950 found in PRONI which include starting date, and in some cases, leaving date; pupil's religion (RC - Roman Catholic, P-Presbyterian, EC (Established Church) or Irish Church – later known as C of I, Church of Ireland, M - Methodist); the number attending in a given year, if available; if pupils came from another school and any fees paid during the pupil's time at school. Pupils are included according to their address or townland.

Information varied, however, in some cases from source to source. For example the year given for the child to start school may not agree with the census (1901, 1911) The census also shows that not all children are recorded in the school rolls, as not all rolls are available.

In brackets are the fathers occupation, or if the mother was a widow, or the child an orphan. When information on occupations stopped, local sources were used.
Those who supplied information on pupils or addresses are shown in brackets.

Sch – School

Pupils attending 1865-1910

Bolies

1905: **Robert Smyth** P (farmer)

Kittybane

1889: **John Armstrong** P (widow)   fees 2s 6d left 1895

1891: **Robert R Lynch** P (farmer) fees 3s left 1896

1909 **Catherine (Cassie) Gillespie** RC (labourer) **John Toland** RC (labourer)

1910 James Toland RC (labourer) **Neil Gillespie** RC (labourer)

Greerstown

1903 Lizzie Boyle RC (scutcher) **Jeannie Boyle** RC (scutcher) both came from Greerstown Sch **John Boyle** RC (scutcher)

Newbuildings

1867 Margaret McCloskey RC (scutcher) aged 9,left 28[th]March 1874

1868 Eliza Jane McCloskey RC (scutcher) aged 7, left on 7th Aug 1875

1869 Emma Lizzie Henry P (shopkeeper) **Sarah McDevitt** RC (shopkeeper) aged 7 in 1878? Fees 66s 8d **Mary A and Bridget McLenahan** RC (labourer) **Maggie McKeever** RC (shopkeeper) –may also have owned the public house-family name may have changed to McIvor . The family moved to Quigleys Point in 1890's **Bridget McLaughlin** RC (shopkeeper) **Maggie Parkhill** RC (labourer) **Jeanie and Lizzie McGregor** P (clerk) **Mary McGarron** P (cow dealer) **Mary McCloskey** RC (scutcher) **Fanny McClenahan** RC (scutcher) **Jeannie (Jane?) Devine** RC (shoemaker) aged 7 in 1876? fees 12s 8d in 1878 her age is recorded as 11 and fees 50s 3d and address given as Ballyarten, left 17th March 1883

1870 Hugh Devine RC (scutcher) also a **Hugh Devine** RC (shoemaker) aged 7, fees 12s 61/2 d left 1880**John Devine** RC (shoemaker) aged 9

1872 William McCloskey RC (scutcher) **Susan McKeever** RC (shopkeeper/publican) **Annie Smyth** P (labourer) **Cassie Mc Lenahan** P (labourer) **Rebecca Smyth** RC (labourer) **Christine Curry** P (widow) **Samuel McClenahan** RC (scutcher) aged 8, left 1877

1873 Samuel Cunningham C of I (farmer) aged 7, fees 24s 6d left 1878

1874 John Doherty RC (carpenter) from Primity? Aged 7 in 1875, fees 9s 10d left 1878 **Martha Doherty** RC (carpenter) aged 8, fees 3s 4d may have left in 1878 **William James Doherty** RC (carpenter) aged 11, from Killymallaght Sch into 2nd grade left 1877

1875 Tommy Doherty RC (carpenter) **William Orr** aged 10, (clerk) came from Carnamoyle Sch Donegal left 1876 **Susan Mullan** RC (labourer) aged 7 left 2nd Dec

1876 **Agnes McGregor** P (clerk) aged 10, fees 3s 4d from Strabane Nat Sch **Minnie McGregor** P (clerk) aged 8, fees 4s left 2nd Dec 1876

1876 **David Henry P** aged 10, (widow) came from Killymallaght Sch **Douglas Patton** P (carpenter) **Nellie McClenahan** RC (labourer) **James Devine** RC (shoemaker) **Jane McGregor** P (clerk) aged 6, fees 3s 11d from Strabane Nat Sch left 2nd Dec 1876 **Ellen McMurray** P (mechanic) aged 10, fees 2s left 27th March 1877 **Lizzie McMurray** P (mechanic) aged 8, fees 3s left 26th May 1877 **Eliza Logue** C of I aged 7, (labourer) fees 3s 5d left 1884

1877 **Jane Devine** RC (shoemaker) aged 7,fees 12s 8d

1878 **Edward McKeever** aged 9, RC (Shopkeeper/publican) came from Waterside Sch into 2nd grade fees 48s left 1883 **Agnes McKeever** RC (shopkeeper) aged 7, fees 38s 7d **James Devine** RC (shoemaker) aged 6, fees 5s 10d left 1880 **Sarah McDevitt** RC (shopkeeper) aged 7, fees 66s 8d

1879 **Rebecca A McCarter** P (carpenter) **William Mullan** (carpenter) **M.A. Collins** RC (labourer) **Mary Smyth** C of I (labourer)**Bella McCurry** P (blacksmith) **Lizzie Smyth** P (labourer) **Cornelius McDevitt** (shopkeeper) aged 7 in 1880, fees 49s 8d left 1887

1880 **George Gamble** aged 8, C of I (labourer) came from Sandville Sch Co Tyrone left 1881 **Patrick McDevitt** RC (tailor)-also given as farmer in 1882 aged 6, fees 22s 6d left 1887 and readmitted 1889 **Robert Faulkener** Cof I (farmer) came from Earlsgift Sch into 1st Grade fees 2s left 1881 – however a Robert Faulkener is on the rolls in 1891

1882 **William McCarter** aged 11 P (carpenter) came from Killymallaght Sch into 1st Grade fees 2s 10d left 1884 **James McLenahan** RC (labourer) aged 7 in 1884 fees 3s 5d left 1889 **George Smyth** C of I (widow) **Edward McCarter** P (carpenter) aged 9, fees 21s 8d left 1889

1883 **Joseph Curran** RC (lapper) aged 11, fees 13s 8d left 1885

1884 **Mary Phillips** RC (labourer) **Matilda McCloskey** RC (labourer) **Ellen McDevitt** RC (shopkeeper) **Sarah McLenahan** RC (labourer) **Sarah Howard** P (labourer) **Jeanie McKeever** RC (shopkeeper/publican) **Maggie Donnell** RC (labourer) **Mary A Howard** P (labourer) **Maggie Smyth** RC (labourer) **Maggie McCarter** P (carpenter) **Cassie Doherty** P (widow) **William Howard** P (labourer) aged 7 in 1886, fees 6s

6d left 1889 **James McCauley** RC (widow) **William Smyth** C of I (labourer) aged 7 in 1888, fees 7s left 1893 –1885 **Thomas McCarron** P (cow dealer) fees 42s left 1889

1886 **David McCarter** P (carpenter) fees 14s 6d left 1893 **Joseph Colhoun** P (insurance agent)

1887 **John McLenahan** RC (labourer) **George Howard** C of I (labourer) **James McKeever** RC (publican) aged 7, left in 1891 **Thomas Gillespie** RC (widow) aged 7 in 1891, left 1895 **James McClay** P (shoemaker) **William Carlin** RC (labourer) aged 7 in 1891, also described as (widow) left 1892

1888 **Richard Smyth** C of I (labourer) aged 8 in 189, described as (widow) left 1893 **Robert Edgar** P (labourer) aged 7 in 1891, described as (orphan) fees 4s left 1895

1889 **James Curry** P (widow) aged 7, left 1894 **Daniel Moyne** RC (orphan) aged 6, fees 16s 6d left 1895 **James Stewart** C of I (labourer) left 1890 **George Strawbridge** P (blacksmith) aged 6, fees 1s 8d left 1896 on rolls in 1897 aged 13, left 1898

1890 **William J Donnell** RC (labourer) aged 8 in 1894, left 1898 **John Carlin** RC (widow) 1891 **John Smyth** P (labourer)

1892 **Joseph Campbell** RC (farmer) **William Smyth** RC (labourer) **John Donnell** RC (labourer)

1893 **Sarah Smyth** RC (widow) **Bella Lecky** M (labourer) **Catherine Houston** RC (farmer) **Maggie Lynch** RC (labourer) **Maggie Nugent** RC (labourer) **George Smyth** RC (labourer) aged 7 in 1896, described as (widow) left 1899 **William Doherty** RC (orphan) aged 7, left 1898

1894 **Patrick Kerr** RC (publican) aged 6, left 1900 **William Smyth** RC (labourer) aged 7, left 1899

1897 **Joseph Donnell** RC (labourer)

1898 **William Burke** RC (engineer) aged 7, into 2nd Grade left 1900 **Sarah and Cassandra Burke** RC (engineer) came from Carrickenavean Co Down on 26th September. The father of this family may have worked on the new railway which ran through Newbuildings to Strabane via Cullion Donemana and Ballymagorry which was completed in 1900 (see In the Shadow of the Tail of the Fox p165) **Francis Phillips** RC (labourer) also given as (widow) aged 7, left 1907 **John Duddy** RC (orphan) aged 6, left 1905 **Francis Strawbridge** (blacksmith) aged 6, left 1904

1899 **Thomas Houston** RC (farmer) **John Miller** P (blacksmith) aged 6, left 1907

1900 **Annie McCan** P (labourer) **Susan Campbell** C of I (quarryman) **Martha McGowan** P (Insurance agent) **Patrick Burke** RC (ganger) aged 6, came on 30th June and left on 11[th]August **James McCloskey** RC aged 6, (labourer) left 1907 **Robert Moyne** RC (orphan) aged 7, left 1905

1903 **Samuel Campbell** P (orphan)

1904 **Maggie Cunningham** P (widow), **Mary McCloskey** R C (labourer)

1905 **George Cunningham** C of I (widow) came from Bready School aged 9, left 2nd July 1906 **John Burn** RC (orphan) **John Donnell** RC (labourer) aged 7, left 8th July 1911

1906 **Thomas Mooney** C of I (orphan) aged 7, left 15th May 1915 **Neil Kerr** RC (merchant) left 30th April 1910 **Frank Browne** RC (labourer) left 25th April 1914

1908 **Charles McGowan** aged 7, P (insurance agent) came from Model Sch aged 7, left 30th Oct 1909 **Bernard Murray** RC (labourer) **Charles Murray** RC (labourer) **Robert Murray** RC (labourer) aged 7, left 12th Nov 1910

1909 **Winnie McLaughlin** RC (tailor) **Dan McLaughlin** RC (tailor)

1910 **Albert Millar** P (blacksmith) aged 6, left 3rd May 1913 **Patrick Donnell** RC (labourer) aged 8, left 10th July 1915

Primity

1869 **Jane Rea** P (labourer) aged 7 in 1874? Fees 6s 2d left 21st Nov 1882 **Mary White** RC (orphan) left 13th Feb 1875

1871 **Samuel Cunningham** C of I (farmer) **Rebecca Cunningham** C of I (farmer) aged 7, fees 25s 6d **James Collins** RC (labourer) aged 12 **Daniel Collins** RC (labourer) aged 9

1872 **Robert Cunningham** C of I (farmer) aged 6 in 1875, fees 34s 6 d left 1881 **Ducilla Orr** P (mason) **Bella Phillips** RC (labourer)

1874 **William James Doherty** RC (carpenter) came from Killymallaght Sch

1876 **Isabella McCorkell** P (farmer) aged 14, fees 6s left 14ᵗʰ June 1877

1879 **Fannie Armstrong** P (widow) **Bella Tedlie?** P (blacksmith)

1881 **David McCorkell** P (farmer) aged 11, fees 24s 2d left 1885

1882 **Robert Armstrong** P (widow) aged 8, fees 13s 1d left 1888

1883 **Joseph Orr** aged 8 (mason) came from Clooney Trc Sch fees 10d **William Orr** P (mason) left 1889 **John Phillips** aged 9, RC (labourer) came from Greerstown Sch 12s 1d left 1886 **George Smyth** C of I (widow) aged 6, fees 18s 11d left 1887

1884 **William Armstrong** P (widow) aged 7 in 1887, fees 5s 6d left 1893 **Jane McCutcheon** P (labourer) **Lizzie McCutcheon** P (labourer) **Joseph Henry** P (widow) fees 20s 1d left 1886

1890 **James Lynch** P (farmer) – a James Lynch is recorded aged 9 in 1880 and leaving in 1882 also a James Lynch aged 8 in 1894 leaving 1896 ? **Robert Lynch** P (labourer) aged 7 in 1890, left 1896 –a Robert Lynch C of I (labourer) also from Primity aged 6 in 1896, left 1898 ?

1891 **William J Doherty** (orphan) RC **James McGrory** RC (labourer)

1893 **Rebecca Lynch** P (labourer) **Mary McNamee** RC (labourer) **Mary Moyne** RC (widow)-lived with an aunt- a seamstress) **Nellie (Ellen) Hegarty** RC (orphan) –Ellen was born in 1896?-lived with orphans Wm Doherty and John Duddy in the home of Jane McGinley a widow **Susan McGrory** RC (labourer)-later of Dam Row? **Daniel McGrory** RC (labourer) – McGrory address also Gortinure

1894 **John McCutcheon** P (labourer) aged 6 in 1896, left 1903

1895 **Thomas McDonald** P (mason) came from Greerstown Sch aged 7 into 1ˢᵗ Grade, left 1897 **John MCCorkell** P (mason) also described as (farmer) aged 5 in 1896, left 1902 **John Duddy** RC (orphan)

1896 **Joseph Lynch** P (labourer) aged 7 in 1898, left 1900

1898 **James McCloskey** RC (labourer)

1899 **Michael Lynch** P (labourer) aged 8 in 1901, left 1906 **Robert Moyne** RC (widow) -lived with aunt a seamstress) **John Lynch** P (labourer) aged 8, left 1905

1900 **Alex McNamee** aged 11, (labourer) came from Strabane Sch into 3ʳᵈ Grade left 1901 **Joseph McNamee** aged 7, (labourer) came from Strabane Sch into Infants left 1901 **Maggie Moyne** RC (labourer)- –she is 2 in 1901? **Minnie McDermott** P (shoemaker) **Sarah (Sadie) Brown** RC (labourer) **William McCloskey** RC (labourer) **Lizzie (Eliza?) McCloskey** RC (labourer) **Sarah McGrory** RC (labourer)- may later have lived in Dam Row **Marianne McGrory** RC (labourer) **Maggie McCloskey** RC (labourer) –she was born in 1900 **Mary Devlin** RC (labourer)

1901 **Daniel Sharkey** aged 9, RC (labourer) came from Killymallaght Sch on 13th May and left on 29th June

1904 **Rose Brown** RC (farmer) -Rose is 9 in 1911 census **John Loughrey** RC (labourer) came from Ballougry Sch into 2nd Grade left 4th Mar 1905 **Robert Henry** C of I (labourer) aged 6, left 4th Sept 1909

1907 **Andrew Walker** P (carpenter) came from Strand Sch left 17th Feb 1912 **Hugh Browne** RC (farmer)

1908 **James Devlin** RC

1909 **Jeannie McDermott** P (shoemaker) **Josephine Browne** RC (farmer) **Joseph Henry** C of I (labourer) aged 10, left 27th Feb 1915

1910 **Sam McDermott** P (shoemaker)

Rossnagalliagh

1865 **William Brown** RC (farmer) age 11, left 1874 **Francis Curry** RC (farmer) in 1867 aged 11, left 1880 **Bessie Crawford** P (farmer) came on 11 th Sept

1866 **Bella Crawford** P aged 11 (farmer) left on 12th May 1877 fees paid 12s0d **Eliza J Crawford** P (farmer) aged 9, fees paid 37s 0d

1867 **John James Brown** RC (farmer) aged 10, fees 15s 8d left 1878 **John James Hanna** P (farmer) aged 9, fees 1s 3d

1868 **Margaret Crawford** P (farmer) aged 7, fees paid 28s 3 ½d **Bella Logue** C of I (labourer) aged 9, fees paid 1s 6d **Hugh Brown** RC (farmer) aged 10 - in 1874 recorded as age 14, left 1875 or 1876

1869 **Mary Brown** RC (farmer) aged 7 in 1874, fees 33s 9d left 6th Dec 1879 **Lizzie Brown** RC (farmer) in 1874 she is aged 6?, fees 39s 5d left 2nd Dec 1876 **Eliza**

Smyth C of I (labourer) aged 7 in 1875?, fees 20s 9 ½ d left 15th Nov 1879 **Matilda Smyth** C of I (labourer) **Maggie Hanna** P (farmer) **John Curry** RC (farmer) in 1861 recorded as age 13, left 1874 **Elizabeth** (Eliza?) **Logue** C of I (labourer) aged 7 in 1878?, fees 3s 5d left 27th Dec 1884 **Sarah McCloskey** RC (labourer) **Sarah Jane Smyth** C of I (labourer) aged 7, left 6th Nov 1875 **Margaret Smyth** C of I (labourer) aged 7, fees 4s left 14th Oct 1876 **Francis Brown** RC (farmer) **Ellen Browne** RC (farmer) aged 8 in 1869, fees 10s left 11 Jan 1879 **Sarah Hanna** P (farmer) aged 7, fees 38s 11d left 24th Sept 1881

1871 **Samuel Brown** RC (farmer) aged 7 in 1873, fees 18s 7d left 1881 **David Logue** C of I (labourer) aged 9 in 1875, fees 4s left 1881 **William Ward** RC (farmer) aged 14

1872 **James Crawford** (farmer) aged 6 in 1874, fees 50s 8d left 1883 – also given as age 13 in 1882 and 19s 6d fees and leaving in 1884 **Alexander Logue** C of I (labourer) **Robert Hanna** P (farmer) aged 6 in 1875, fees 27s 6 ½ d left 1882

1873 **Patrick Brown** RC (farmer) aged 7 in 1876, fees 54s 2d left 1883 – also on rolls 1884 aged 13 fees 21s 5d left 1885 **David Millar** C of I (widow) **John Browne** RC (farmer) aged 7 in 1876, fees 45s 7d left 1883-in 1884 John Browne was again on the rolls aged 13 fees 13s 10d left 1885 **Thomas J Brown** RC (farmer) recorded as 6 in 1878? fees 38s 3d left 1885 –on 8th May 1886 Thomas is on rolls aged 14 fees 4s 10d and left on 5th June 1886 **John Wilson** C of I (labourer)

1874 **William McCloskey** RC (labourer) aged 6 ½, fees 23s 4d left 1881 or 19th May 1882 **Mary Brown** RC (farmer) aged 7 fees 33s 9d left on 6th Dec 1879 **Lizzie Brown** RC (farmer) aged 6, fees 39s 5d left 2nd Dec 1876

1875 **Robert Wilson** C of I (labourer) aged 11 fees 10s 7d left 1880 **Eliza Smyth** C of I (labourer) aged 7, fees 20s 9d left 15th Nov 1879

1876 **Michael Doherty** aged 8, RC (dealer) came from St Columbs Sch went into 1st Year left 1877 **Kate McMennin** RC (orphan) aged 14, fees 16s 3d came from Strabane Sch left 4th Aug 1883 **David Miller** P (widow) aged 6, fees 55s 1d left 1882

1877 **David Crawford** P (farmer) aged 6 in 1880? fees 54s 81/2 d left 1886 **Mary McCloskey** (labourer) aged 7, fees 16s left 11th Dec 1880 **Robert Smyth** P (labourer) aged 7, fees 54s 61/2 d left 1883

1879 **Agnes Barr** P (farmer)   **Sarah Brown** RC (farmer) **Agnes McCloskey** RC (labourer) **William Carlyle** aged 9 P (shopkeeper) came from Longfields Sch Yorkshire left 1884

1881 **John Wilson** P (labourer) aged 10,   fees 8s left 1886 **Robert Osborne** P (labourer) aged 10, fees 7s 9d left 1885

1882 **Charles McFaul** RC (farmer) aged 8, came from Cross Clonmaney Sch Co Donegal fees 53s 9d left 1888 **Bernard Mc Faul** RC (farmer) aged 7, came from Cross Clonmaney Sch Co Donegal 28s 4d left 1888

1883 **William Browne** RC (farmer) aged 6 in 1884, fees 43s 2d left 1890   **John McFaul** RC (farmer) aged 7 in 1884, fees 82s 2d left 1888

1884 **Matilda Lynch** P (labourer) **Mary Warde** RC (farmer) **Martha Kilgore** P (labourer) **Agnes Browne** RC (farmer) **James Browne** RC (farmer) aged 6 in 1885, fees 55s 11d left 1892 in rolls 29th April 1893 aged 14 left in 1894 **James Lynch** RC (labourer) aged 6 in 1886, fees 10s left 1891 **Robert Lynch** P (labourer) aged 6 in 1888, left 1893 **Susan MC Closkey** RC (labourer) –born 1884? **Ellen MCloskey** RC (labourer) born 1886? **Bridget McCloskey** RC (labourer) **John Lynch** P (labourer) aged 6 in 1890, left 1893 **John McGinnis** P (labourer) aged 6, fees 6s left 1896

1887 **George McCloskey** RC (labourer) aged 7,   fees 4s 6d left 1893

1889 **John Deehan** RC (orphan) came from Limerick into 2nd year,   left 1891

1890 **James Curry** aged 10, RC (harness maker) came on 25 th August and left on 25th Oct 1890 **John McCloskey** RC (labourer) aged 6, left 1896

1893 **Lizzie Jarvis** C of I (labourer) **Mary N Elliot** RC (farmer) daughter of principal and later teacher in the school;- this is Mary's birth date; **Jessie Campbell** P (farmer)- a Bessie Campbell is born in this year-same person? **Jeannie Morrison** P (labourer) **Sarah Browne** RC (farmer) **Hannah Doherty** RC (labourer) **Margaret Elliot** RC (farmer) -daughter of the Principal; **Mary Browne** RC (farmer) she is 14 in 1911 census- **Lizzie Porter** C of I (labourer) **Michael Ward** RC (farmer) **William I Sweeny** RC (labourer) aged 7 in 1893, left 1895

1894 **Hugh Devine** RC (labourer) aged 6, left 1900

1897 **Wm G Browne** RC (widow) aged 7,came from Rosemount Sch–left 1903 a brother of Catherine (Cassie aged 11 and Hugh aged 10. They lived with an uncle-

James Brown (farmer)

1898 **John Campbell** P (farmer) aged 6 in 1901, left 1909

1899 **Charles Doherty** RC (labourer) aged 10, came from Managhbeg /Mullaghbeg? Sch on 30th Jan and left 8th May **William Doherty** aged 8, RC (labourer) from Managhbeg?Mullagbeg Sch left 1900 **Maggie Doherty** RC (labourer) came from Mullaghbeg Sch **John Browne** RC (carter) also given as (farmer) aged 5 in 1900, left 1907

1900 **Maggie Browne** RC – a Margaret Browne is 1 in 1901 (see census) same person? **William McGaviagn** aged 10, RC (labourer) came from Greerstown Sch left 1906 **James McGavigan** aged 13 RC (labourer) came from Greerstown Sch left 1903 **Andrew Campbell** P (farmer) aged 5 left 1910 **Catherine (Cassie) Brown** RC (cattle dealer/farmer –she lived with an uncle) –Catherine was born in 1900 –in rolls she is living at Ballyore

1901 **James C Stewart** aged 8, P (widow) came from Ladies Sch on 11th March left on 10th August **Jeanie Stewart** P (widow) came from Ladies Sch Londonderry

1902 **Michael Campbell** P (farmer)

1903 **John Browne** RC (orphan) came from St Columbs Male Sch aged 9 into 2nd year, left 1910

1904 **Mollie Stewart** P (policeman) **George Campbell** P (farmer) **Willie Browne** RC (orphan) aged 6, left 2nd Sept 1911 **Dan McGavigan** RC (labourer) aged 7, left 12th Oct 1910

1905 **Patrick Browne** RC (farmer) left 9th May 1914 **Richard Campbell** P (farmer) aged 7, left 8th Oct 1910

1906 **George Campbell** P (farmer) aged 5, left 21st Feb 1914 **Robert Stewart** P (policeman) aged 6, left 27th Feb 1915

1908 **Hugh Browne** RC (orphan) aged 7, left 25th April 1914 **Patrick Moyne** RC (labourer)

1909 **Molly Moyne** RC (labourer) **Lizzie Moyne** RC (labourer) **Mary McGowan** P (labourer) **Maggie Gillespie** RC (labourer) **James Campbell** P (widow) also labourer-aged 8, left 1st May 1915

1910 **Josie McGowan** P (labourer)

Lower Tully

1868 **Richard Ferry** P (farmer) aged 15 left 1874 **Samuel Ferry** P (farmer) aged 15 left 1874

1869 **Martha Doherty** P (labourer) **Lizzie McCarter** P (merchant)-she may have lived in Tully House later Kennedys.) **Sarah Devine** RC (labourer) **Annie Jarvis** P (labourer) **Annie Lynch** P (labourer) **Annie Devine** RC (labourer) age 7 in 1877? fees 20s left 11th Dec 1880 **Mary Anne Torry** P (farmer) aged 17? left 23rd July 1874

1871 **Alexander McClay** P (labourer) aged 7 in 1873, fees 39s 7d (this might be an error in fees as it seems too much) left 1878 **Bessie Torry** P (farmer) aged 10 fees 12s 6d **Cassie Torry** P (farmer) aged 8 fees 14s **David Lynch** P (labourer) aged 9, left 1877

1872 **George McCarter** P (merchant) aged 10 in 1876, came from Derry Female Sch fees 27s 3d left 1880 **Robert Lynch** (labourer) in 1875 aged 7, left 1880

1873 **Jane McClay** P (labourer) aged 12, left 23rd May 1874

1874 **Mary McClay** P (labourer) aged 11, left 24th July 1875

1875 **James McClay** P (labourer) aged 7, fees 7s left 1879 **Mary Devine** RC (labourer) **Jane Lynch** P (labourer) **Mike Gallagher** aged 9, RC came from Glendermott Sch into 1st Grade, left 1876 **Catherine Jarvis** P (labourer) aged 7, fees 25s 9d left on 15th Nov 1879

1876 **Catherine A McClay** P (labourer) aged 8, fees 2s left 25th Aug 1877 **Catherine A Lynch** P (labourer) aged 7, fees 17s 4d left 11th Dec 1880

1877 **Maggie Doherty** P (labourer) aged 7, fees 17s 3d left 27th Oct 1883 **Annie Devine** RC (labourer) aged 7, fees 20s left 1880

1878 **Jeanie McCarter** P (merchant) aged 8 **Annie McCarter** P (merchant) aged 14, left 6th Dec 1879 **Cassie McCarter** P (merchant) aged 12, fees £4 16s 11d- probably for all the McCarter girls - left on 15th Nov 1879 **Stephen Lynch** P (labourer) aged 6, fees 12s 10d left 1883

1879 Annie Doherty P (labourer) **Isabella Ferris** C of I (labourer) **John Devine** RC

(labourer) aged 6 in 1882? fees 7s 3d left 1884 **Mary Devine** RC (labourer)

1880 Andrew Jervis C of I (labourer) in 1882 aged 7, fees 8d left 1884

1881 James Devine RC (labourer) aged 6 in 1884, fees 4s 10d left 1889

1882 Robert A Gamble P (farmer) aged 6 in 1884 fees 36s 5d left 1891 **William I Doherty** P (labourer) aged 6 in 1884, fees 42s 2d left 1891on 1892 rolls aged 14 left 1893

1884 Grace Devine RC (labourer) **Anne Strawbridge** P (labourer) **Cassie Parkhill** RC (labourer) **Rose Devine** RC (labourer) **Mary Parkhill** RC (labourer) **Annie Galbraith** P (farmer) **Robert Parkhill** RC (labourer) aged 7 in 1886, fees 3s 6d left 1892 **Joseph Doherty** P (labourer) aged 7 in 1887, fees 7s left 1895

1887 William (Willie) Jervis C of I (labourer) aged 6 in 1888, fees 3s left 1890 **Abram Doherty** P (labourer) aged 7 in 1890, left in 1891

1891 Thomas Jervis C of I (labourer) in 1892 aged 6, left 1896

1892 Hugh Devine RC (labourer)

1893 Minnie Creighton Cof I (labourer) **Sarah Dunne** P (labourer) –Sarah Jane Dunn was born in 1892 –see 1901 census

1898 William G Creighton C of I (labourer) called George? aged 7, came on 30th June and left on 11th August **Elizabeth Creighton** C of I (labourer) came from Ballougry Sch on 6th October

1900 David Dunne aged 8, P (labourer) came from Bready School where he is recorded to start on 13th June 1898 and have lived in Gortivea-he returned to Bready Sch on 5th October 1901 aged 9 **Agnes Lynch** RC (labourer) **Sara Lynch** RC (labourer) **David Browne** P (labourer) came from Bready Sch left 1901

1903 Samuel Clements M (farmer)

1904 Maggie Clements M (farmer) **Lizzie Lynch** RC (labourer) **Maud Clements** M (farmer)

1906 Willie Lynch RC (labourer) left 2nd May 1914

1907 **William Logue** C of I aged 9, (labourer) came from Greerstown Sch – a William Logue came from Tirkeeveny aged 5 in 1901 census –same one?-left 25ᵗʰ Sept 1909 **Willie Clements** M (farmer) aged 6, left 11ᵗʰ May 1914 **David Murray** aged 7, left 12ᵗʰ Oct 1910

1910 **Jack Clements** M (farmer) left 1ˢᵗ May 1915

Clampernow/Upper Tully

1870 **Martha Smyth** C of I (labourer) aged 12, fees 11s left 20ᵗʰ Jan 1877 **Archibald (Archie) Smyth** P (farmer) aged 8

1873 **Alexander Smyth** P (farmer)aged 6 in 1874, fees 51s 6d in 1882 fees 21s 2d left 16ᵗʰ Sept 1882

1874 **L Smyth** P (labourer)

1876 **Willie Smyth** P (farmer) age 6 in 1877, fees 73s 9d left 1882

1879 **Bella McDermott** P (labourer) **Benjamin Logan** P (labourer) aged 7, came on 18ᵗʰ July left on 20ᵗʰ Dec 1879

1886 **George Strawbridge** P (labourer) aged 7 in 1889, fees 14s 6d left 1895

1888 **James Strawbridge** P (labourer) aged 7 in 1891, left 1897

1900 **Margaret Walker** P (labourer)

1906 **Daniel Murray** RC (labourer) **Joseph Walker** P (labourer) left 23ʳᵈ Jan 1915

1908 **Archie Smyth** P (widow) aged 5,   left 18ᵗʰ July 1914   **Irene Smyth** P (widow)

1909 **Agnes Walker** P (labourer) **Jeanie Doherty** P (labourer) **Eveline (Evelyn) Walker** P (labourer)

Magheramason Co Tyrone

1869 **Annie Campbell** Cof I (labourer) **Matilda Osborne** P (labourer) aged 7 in 1875? fees 1s 4d left 6ᵗʰ Jan 1877 **Jane Osborne** P (labourer) aged 7 in 1877? Fees 2s 3d left on 5ᵗʰ Jan 1878 **Minnie McNeely** P (farmer) **Jane Kelly** C of I (labourer) aged 7 in 1875? left 1ˢᵗ May 1878 **Martha McCourt** P (labourer) aged 7 in 1876?

Fees 5s 1d left 20th Dec 1879

1873 **William Kelly** C of I (labourer) aged 7 in 1878? Fees 4s 3d left 1880 -a William Kelly from Tamnaclare (or Clare) came from Rossnagalliagh Sch to Bready on 6th Dec 1880 aged 11-was it the same person ? **Matilda Kelly** C of I (labourer) aged 8 **Edgar Andrew** or **Edgar John Hall** P (labourer) aged 7 left 1875

1874 **Matilda Lynch** P (widow) aged 13, left on 13th Feb 1875

1875 **William Lynch** RC (shoemaker) fees 16s 31/2 d left 1880 **Matilda Osborne** P (labourer) aged 7, fees 1s 4d left 6th Jan 1877 **James Campbell** C of I (labourer) aged 7 in 1878, fees 8s 4d left 1881 (is recorded as living in Rossnagalliagh in 1878)

1877 **John McNeely** P (farmer) aged 7 in 1878, fees 63s 10d left 1885 **Jane Osborne** P (labourer) aged 7, fees 2s 3d left 1878

1878 **Bessie Gamble** P (farmer) did Bessie live at The Woods, in an area called The Cooley came to school on November 18th address is also given as Coolgmaghery aged 12, fees 46s 4d

1879 **Lizzie McCourt** P (labourer) **Lizzie McNeely** P (farmer) went to Bready Sch on 22nd May 1888 aged 10 **Martha McNeely** P (farmer) went to Bready Sch on 22nd May 1888 aged 12 **William McNeely** P (farmer) aged 6 in 1881, fees 44s 8d went to Bready Sch on 21st November 1887 aged 13 – in Rossnagalliagh records left 1888; **Sarah Love** P (sexton of Magheramason Presbyterian Church) came from Bready Sch on 18th February 1879 and paid 1 shilling 6 pence a week; **Sarah McCorkell** P (labourer) **John J Lynch** P (labourer) came on 16th July and left on 10th Dec 1879

1882 **James McCorkell** P (labourer) **Francis Logue** C of I (labourer) aged 8, fees 3d left 1885

1883 **William MCCorkell** P (labourer) aged 6 in 1884, fees 13s 5d left 1892 in school rolls on 19thApril 1893 aged 16 left 22nd July 1893

1884 **William Colhoun** P aged 10, (insurance agent) came from Carlisle Road Sch fees 16s 1d left 1888 **Robert Colhoun** P aged 8, (insurance agent) came from Carlisle Road Sch fees 15s 8d left 1888 **Matthew Colhoun** P (insurance agent)

1886 **Joseph McCorkell** C of I (labourer) aged 7 in 1889, fees 11s left 1895 **William Love** P (sexton of Magheramason Presbyterian Church) aged 8 in 1888, fees 12s 6d left 1893

1887 **Andrew McNeely** P (farmer) went to Bready Sch on 22nd May 1888 may have returned to Rossnagalliagh and then returned to Bready on 23rd Jan 1897 aged 15? **Robert Campbell** P (labourer) aged 6 in 1889,   fees 4s left 1893

1888 **William Campbell** P aged 12, (labourer) came from Bready Sch fees 2s left 1889 **John Campbell** P (labourer) aged 13 left 1889

1891 **George McCorkell** C of I (labourer) aged 6 in 1893,   left 1899

1893 **Mary Love** P (labourer) – a Mary Love went to Bready Sch on 4th March 1901 (b 22nd Feb 1891) same person?

1900 **Maggie Doherty** P (labourer) **Greta Osborne** P (labourer) **Rebecca McCorkell** C of I (labourer)

1904 **Evelyn Caskey** (daughter of Rev Caskey Minister of Magheramason Presbyterian Church)

1905 **John (Jack) Caskey** aged 7, P (Presbyterian minister) came from Bready Sch into 1st yr left 13th June 1908

1906 **Willie Love** P (labourer) aged 12 came from Clooney Trc Sch left 25th April 1907

1907 **Bertie Caskey** P (Presbyterian Minister)

1909 **Katie Doherty** P (labourer) **Alex Logue** C of I (labourer)

1910 **Willie McNeely** P (farmer)

Gortin (or Gorton)

1872 **Ellen Tosh** P (labourer)

1874 **Cassie Doherty** P (labourer) aged 11, left 6th Nov 1875

1875 **B Doherty** P (labourer) **William Elder** P (labourer) recorded as coming from Newbuildings National School? Fees 17s 11/2 d left

1880 **Charles Elder** P (labourer) aged 8 from Newbuildings Nat Sch? fees 12s 6d

1876 **Martha Elder** P (labourer) aged 7, fees 22s 10d left 6th Nov 1880

1877 **John Tosh** P (labourer) aged 7, fees 46s 7d left 1883

1878 **John Godfrey** P (labourer) **Bessie Elder** P (labourer) aged 7, fees 19s 5d **Martha Godfrey** P (labourer) aged 12, left 19th March 1879 **Cassie Godfrey** P (labourer) aged 10, fees 6d left 19th March 1879 **Ellen Godfrey** P (labourer) aged 8, left 19th March 1879

1880 **William McCloskey** P aged 8 (coachman) came from Clooney Trc Sch into 2nd Grade fees 2s 7d came on 2nd June and left on 18th Dec 1880 **Samuel Elder** P (labourer) aged 7 in 1881, fees 23s 4d left 1887- in 1888 rolls Samuel is aged 14 fees 6s 5d and left 1890 **Samuel Clark** P (labourer) aged 7, fees 24s 10d left 1885

1882 **William Lynch** aged 9, P (labourer) from Killymallaght Sch fees 13s left 1885 **Lizzie Lynch** came from Killymallaght Sch **William I Tosh** P (labourer) aged 6, fees 16s 4d left 1888 **Robert Curry** P (widow) aged 7 in 1885, fees 17s left 1890

1884 **Janie Walsh** of Gortin Hall (farmer) **Maggie Keys** P (labourer) **Sarah Colhoun** P (labourer) **Michael Lynch** P (labourer) aged 7 in 1886, fees 1s left 1889 **William Colhoun** P (labourer) **Thomas Elder** P (labourer) aged 7 in 1887, fees 7s 2d left 1890

1886 **William Little** P (labourer) aged 10, from Sandville Sch fees 9s 1d left 1889 **Maggie Little** (Lyttle) came from Sandville Sch Co Tyrone **Robert Colhoun** P (labourer) aged 6 in 1888, fees 4s 6d left 1893 **James Curry** P (widow)

1887 **Charles Lynch** P (labourer)

1891 **Thomas Colhoun** P (labourer)

1892 **Alex Elder** P (labourer) aged 7 in 1884, fees 31s 5d left 1889

1893 **Mary Keys** P (labourer) **Letita Curry** P (labourer) **Minnie Murray** RC (labourer) **Lizzie Murray** RC (labourer) **David Keys** P (labourer) aged 10, from Killymallaght Sch left 1897

1894 **John E Walsh** P (farmer) Gortin Hall

1895 **David Strawbridge** P (labourer) aged 7 in 1898, left 1900

1898 **William I Strawbridge** P (labourer) **Robert Curry** P (labourer) aged 9, left 1899 **Andrew Curry** P (labourer) aged 10, came on 30th April and left 5th November 1898

1899 **Samuel Patterson** aged 10, P (labourer) came from Oghill Public Elementary Sch into 2nd year left 1900 **William Patterson** aged 8, P (labourer) came from Oghill Sch into 1st Grade left 1900

1901 **Harry (Henry?) Curry** P (labourer)

1905 **Robert Murray** RC (labourer)

1906 **Willie Moore** P (labourer) aged 10, came from Clooney Trc Sch into 2nd grade left 27th Feb 1912 **John I McCormac** RC (labourer)

1909 **Ellen Olphert** C of I (labourer) **Mary McGinnis** C of I (labourer)

Ballyorr

1867 **Matilda Jane Orr** P (farmer) aged 12, left 10th Jan 1874 **Catherine Orr** P (farmer) aged 10, fees 5s left 1st May 1878

1869 **Violet Christy** P (farmer) **Lizzie Hyndman** P (farmer) **Bella Maria Orr** P (farmer)

1872 **Matilda McCarron** P (cow dealer) **Rebecca Hyndman** P (farmer)

1873 **William Hyndman** P (farmer) aged 6 in 1874 fees 32s 11d in 1882 extra fees 5s 3d left 1884

1874 **George Orr** P (farmer) aged 7 in 1878? fees 36s 8d left 1884

1875 **Joseph Henry** P (labourer) -in 1877 was recorded as (widow) fees 35s 81/2d left 1883 **Jessie Orr** P (farmer) **Maria B Orr** P (farmer) aged 6, fees 46s 41/2 d left 25th Dec 1880 -Christmas Day? **Mary Jane Henry** P (farmer) aged 8, from Killymallaght Sch fees 28s 6d left 2nd July1881

1876 **Willie Lynch** RC (shoemaker) aged 6 in 1878, fees 39s 2d left 1886 – in 1886 Willie is recorded as aged 16 and paid fees of 27s **Elizabeth J McCarron** P (cow dealer) aged 8, fees 3s 2d left 27th Oct 1877 **Matilda Lynch** P (farmer) aged 12, fees 6s 01/2d left on 11th Jan 1879 **David Henry** P (widow) came from Killymallaght Sch fees 30s 4d left 1882

1878 **David Hyndman** P (farmer) aged 7 in 1880, fees 49s 5d left 1887 **James Lynch** P (farmer) fees 7s 10d left 1879

1879 **Andrina Hyndman** P (farmer) **Bella Mary Hyndman** P (farmer)

1880 **John Henry** P (widow) –recorded as 6 in 1882,   fees 21s 7d left 1888

1883 **Thomas McCarron** P (cow dealer)

1884 **Maggie McCarron** P (cow dealer) **Lizzie Doherty** P (widow) **John Hyndman** P (farmer) aged 7 in 1888, (widow) left 1893 **Rose Kerr** RC (carpenter/shopkeeper) Rose is 15 in 1901 **Susan Kerr** RC (shopkeeper) came from St Columbs Female Sch, Waterside **Mary Phillips** RC (labourer)

1885 **Christine Jane Parke** C of I (widow) came from Carrigans Sch Co Donegal on 6th April lived with an uncle, Mr Nixon, a grocer, by 1901

1886 **James Hyndman** P (farmer) aged 7 in 1889, also described as (widow) left 1893 **George McCloskey** RC (labourer)

1887 **George Strawbridge** P (blacksmith) **John McCloskey** RC (labourer)

1891 **Patrick (Pattie) Kerr** RC (shopkeeper)

1893 **Sarah Browne** RC (cattle dealer) - a Sarah Brown is 5 in 1901 census **Jane (Jeanie) Millar** P (blacksmith) **Jane Kerr** RC (publican/shopkeeper) **Catherine (Cassie) Kerr** RC (carpenter/publican) **SarahPhillips** RC (labourer) **Bella J O'Donnell** RC (labourer)-Bella was born in 1895 see 1901 census

1895 **James Lynch** aged 10 C of I (labourer) came from Clooney Trc Sch into 1st grade left 1897 **Charles O'Donnell** RC (labourer) (the family are referred to as Donnell in rolls but O'Donnell in census) **John Millar** P (blacksmith) **Francis Strawbridge** P (blacksmith)

1897 **Robert Millar** P (blacksmith) left 1907 – in 1904 a Bertie Millar P (blacksmith) is aged 7, and left in 1908-same person?

1900 **Lily Hanna** P (labourer) **Mollie Hanna** P (labourer) **John Kerr** RC (shopkeeper)- was this the Kerr family who lived at Dam Row and later beside the Methodist Church? –John was to serve in WW1 in a Cavalry Regiment **Bella Millar** P (blacksmith) **Kate Brown** RC (cattle dealer) – she was born in 1900 **Nellie Browne** RC (labourer) – may be Ellen

1901 **John Brown** RC (labourer)

1903 **Neal Kerr** RC (shopkeeper) **John O'Donnell** RC (labourer) **John Kerr** RC (shopkeeper) aged 6, left 1907

1904 **Mary Browne** RC (labourer) **Minnie Lynch** RC (farmer) **Annie Phillips** RC (orphan) **Willie Porter** C of I aged 8, (labourer) came from Clooney Trc Sch into infants left 4th Oct 1905

1906 **John Porter** C of I (labourer) came from Clooney Trc Sch- left 22nd July 1916 the Porter family lived at Brick Kilns by 1911 (now the home of Jackie Porter, Woodside Road)

1907 **Albert E Millar** P (blacksmith) **Patrick Donnell** (O'Donnell) RC (labourer)

1909 **Susan Mellon** RC (carpenter) **Mary Cunningham** P (widow) **Agnes Browne** RC (labourer) **John P Mellon** RC (carpenter) **Annie Mellon** RC (carpenter) **Elizabeth (Lizzie) Donnell** RC (labourer)

Dunhugh- (also Dunhue)

1871 **Anne Collins** RC (farmer) aged 1, left 10th Jan 1874

1879 **Matilda Daly** (widow)

1880 **William J Abram** P (farmer) aged 6 in 1881, fees 59s 8d left 1887- in 1888 rolls William is aged 13 fees 14s and left 1889 Abram's farm later owned by Watsons and then Flanagan

1882 **Robert G Abram** P (farmer) aged 7 in 1884, fees 31s 4d left 1889

1884 **Mary I MCCafferty** RC (carpenter)

1887 **James McCafferty** RC (carpenter) aged 7 in 1889, fees 4s 6d left 1895 **William McCafferty** RC (carpenter) aged 8, fees 18s left 1894

1889 **Andrew Morrison** C of I (farmer) aged 9, fees 7s 2d left 1893

1896 **Mary McCafferty** RC (carpenter) **Bridget McCafferty** RC (carpenter) **Lizzie McCafferty** RC (carpenter) came from St Columbs Female Sch Waterside on 27th July

1900 **Bridget Gillespie** RC (labourer) **Jeanie McCan** Cof I (labourer) **Cassie Collins** RC (farmer)

1901 **John McCafferty** RC (Carpenter)

1903 **Robert Henry** P (labourer)

Coolmaghery

1869 **Mary Ann Curry** P (farmer) **Ellen E Curry** P (farmer)

1872 **Rebecca I Thompson** P (labourer)

1877 **John James Lynch** P (labourer) **Matilda Lynch** P (labourer) aged 8, fees 5d came from Bready Sch left 6th Dec 1879 **Lizzie Lynch** P (labourer) aged 10, fees 1s 1d left 15th June 1878

1878 **Bessie Gamble** P (farmer) aged 12, fees 46s 4d

1879 **Matilda Curry** P (farmer)

1884 **Agnes G Irvine** P (farmer) **Agnes Thompson** P (blacksmith)

1886 **Hugh Thompson** P (labourer) aged 6 in 1887, fees 14s 6d left 1894 on rolls 18th May 1895 rolls aged 14, left 13th July 1895 **James Thompson** P (blacksmith) aged 7, fees 24s 10d left 1893

1888 **Alex Irvine** P (shopman) **Maggie Sweeny** RC-Maggie had attended Killymallaght Sch and then Bready Sch aged 7 in 1886 **Robert Tosh** P (labourer) aged 9, fees 1s left 1889

1890 **Alex Thompson** P (blacksmith) **Alexander Barr** P (farmer) aged 7, left 1891

1893 **William Hare** P (farmer) **William Barr** P (farmer) aged 7, left 1899

1894 **Jeanie McCourt** C of I came from Clooney Trc Sch on 10th December

1895 **Patrick Doherty** aged 12, RC (labourer) came from Bready Sch aged 12 into 3rd Grade, left 1897 **Bernard Doherty** RC (labourer) aged 7, 1896 left 1899

1897 **David Barr** P (farmer) aged 7, left 1900

1900 **Sara McGonigle** P (labourer) **Florence McLaughlin** P (chemist) **Nettie McLaughlin** P (chemist) – lived at Coolmaghery House

1901 **Robert Patrick** P aged 14 (farmer) –he attended Castlemellon Sch and Bready Sch in 1898 aged 10 –into 4th year left 1903 **Annie Patrick** P - 8 years old – in 1901 census Annie is 11 went to Castlemellon Sch and on 14th March 1898 to Bready Sch **Ethel Patrick** aged 7 attended Bready Sch on 27th January 1900 **Lizzie Mary Patrick** – 6 years old attended Bready Sch in 1901.**Jeannie Patrick** P (farmer) Ethel and Lizzie had been born in America and returned to Castlemellon before coming to Coolmaghery

1902 **Lizzie Kennedy** P (farmer) came from Bonds Glen Sch on 13th January- a Lizzie Kennedy who had attended Bonds Glen School before Rossnagalliagh went to Bready School aged 12 on 3rd October 1904. In Bready records she lived in Gortmonley

1904 **Martha Doherty** RC (labourer) **Myrtle Moorhead** P (farmer)

1909 **Kathleen Moorhead** P (farmer)

Prehen-

Note the appearance of parents occupation as factory workers/outworkers as seamstresses. Shirt making factories had begun to appear in Londonderry in 1857 when two Scots Tillie and Henderson opened the first factory using steam driven machines for cutting and sewing shirts. By 1891 they employed 1500 in the factory and 3000 as outworkers. (Bardon p.394)

1875 **Margaret Kane or Hone** RC (farmer) aged 13, fees 5s from Glendermott Sch

1877 **Mary McLaughlin** (orphan) aged 11, fees 21s 2d left 6th Nov 1880 – Mary had come from the Workhouse in Waterside, Londonderry

1879 **Mary A McElvenney** P (farmer)

1883 **John Moran** aged 4 RC (mason) came from St Columb's Male Sch Waterside fees 2s came on 9th July 1883 left 15th Dec 1883

1884 **Cassie Porter** C of I (seamstress) **Maggie Porter** C of I (widow) **Lizzie Phillips** RC (labourer)

1893 **Cassie Lynch** P (labourer) **Annie Clements** M (farmer) - Annie was born in 1891 (Census1901) **Jeannie Gillespie** RC (labourer) **Sarah Norris** P (shirt cutter) **Annie Gillespie** RC (labourer)

1895 **John Gillespie** RC (labourer) aged 8, went into 1st year came from Enagh Sch aged 8 in 1896, left 1900 **William Lynch** C of I (labourer)

1896 **George McVerit or McVent** P (tailor)

1899   Annie Lynch P (labourer) came from Ballougry Sch on 9th May

1900 **Hannah Phillips** RC (labourer) **Lizzie Moran** RC (shirtcutter) **William E Mitchell** P (bank manager)

1901 **George Phillips** aged 11 RC (labourer) came from Killymallaght Sch left 1902 **Mary Phillips** came from Killymallaght Sch **James Lynch** P (labourer) aged 7, left 1907

1904 **Lizzie Phillips** RC (labourer) **Annie Moran** RC (shirt cutter)

1906 **Joseph Lynch** P (labourer) aged 7, left 2nd Feb 1911

1908 **Willie Moran** RC (shirt cutter) left 3rd Oct 1908

Magheracannon

Lizzie Crossan RC (labourer) **Maggie Crossan** RC (labourer) from Greerstown School

1877 **Isabella Stuart** P (farmer) came from Greerstown Sch aged 9, fees 51s 10d

1879 **Mary Ann Strawbridge** P (blacksmith) –in Ballyorr by 1901 **Matilda M Stewart** P (farmer) **Annie Stuart** P (farmer)

1884 **Maggie Millar** P (blacksmith) **Minnie Miller** P (blacksmith) **Annie Strawbridge** P (blacksmith) in Ballyorr by 1901 **Lizzie Campbell** C of I (labourer) **Martin Moyne** RC (widow) aged 14, came from Racecourse Road Sch fees 6d left 1885

1892 **Thomas Colhoun** P (labourer) aged 7, left 1898

1897 **David Butler** aged 12, (labourer) came from Grennan Sch, Donegal **Alexander Porter** C of I (labourer) aged 7 in 1898, left 1900 **Richard Porter** C of I (labourer) aged 6 in 1898, left 1900 **David Porter** C of I (labourer) from Grennan Sch came on 30th March and left on 31st Dec 1897 but on rolls of 1905?

1901 **Joseph McCloskey** RC (labourer) aged 6,   left 1907

1903 **Willie McCloskey** RC aged 6, left 1908

1903 **William Colhoun** C of I (labourer)

1905 **George McCloskey** RC (labourer)

1906 **Willie Love** aged 12, came from Clooney Tce. Sch

1908 **Harry Barr** P (labourer)

Brickkilns

1893 **Maggie Taggart** P (farmer) **Mary Taggart** P (farmer) –in 1901 census Maggie is aged 9 and Mary aged 7 **Cassie Lynch** P (labourer) **Rebecca Lynch** P (labourer)

1895 **Robert Lynch** C of I (labourer) **James Lynch** P (labourer)

1899 **Matilda (Tilda or Tillie) Lynch** P (labourer) – Tilda was born in 1900

1900 **Susan Osbourne** P (labourer)

1901 **William Lynch** P (labourer) aged 7, left 1908

1903 **Joseph Lynch** P (labourer)

1904 **Bella Burke** P (labourer) - aged 12, never attended school before **Jane (Jeanie) Burke** P (labourer) **Mary Burke** P (labourer) – Burke's address may be Prehen

1909 **Robert Burke** P (Labourer)

Craigtown

1893 **Susan Doherty** RC (labourer)

1907 **Martha Doherty** RC (labourer)

1908 **Susan Osbourne** P (labourer) same Susan as in Brick Kilns in 1900?

Creaghcor

Kate Allen P (labourer)

Gortinure

1871 **Sarah Crumley** RC (farmer) aged 9, fees 15s 10d left 29th March 1879

1874 **Daniel Crumley** (farmer) aged 7 in 1877, fees 27s 11/2 d left 1881

1877 **Eliza Anne Kearney** aged 8, (orphan) fees 5s 9d left 20th Oct 1882

1887 **Daniel Moyne** RC (labourer)

1892 **William McGowan** C of I (orphan) came from Killymallaght Sch aged 11, left 1895

1894 **James McGrory** RC aged 7, left 1899

1896 **Daniel McGrory** RC (labourer) aged 7 left 1900

1904 **Ellen Houston** RC (labourer)

1905 **Robert Crumley** RC (farmer) aged 9, left 11th Sept 1909 **Millar Houston** RC (labourer) aged 10, left 6th Oct 1906

1906 **Daniel Crumley** RC (farmer) aged 6, left 26th Nov 1910 **James J Crumley** RC (farmer) **Patrick Crumley** RC (farmer) aged 8, left 18th Feb 1911

1909 **David Porter** C of I (farmer) aged 4, left 1st July 1916

1910 **Maggie Crumley** RC (farmer)

Drumagor

1904 **Nellie Doherty** C of I (labourer)

1906 **James Doherty** C of I (labourer) came from Killmallaght Sch aged 13 **William Doherty** C of I (labourer) aged 13 (twins?) came from Killymallaght Sch left 17th April 1909

Kerry Co Tyrone

1882 **Maggie Coulter** P (carpenter) **Cassie Coulter** P (carpenter) originally lived at Gortivey and attended Bready Sch –Maggie started Bready 1st July 1879 aged 6 and came to Rossnagalliagh in March 1881 Cassie began Bready Sch 7th October 1879 and came to Rossnagalliagh on 4th November 1882

1883 **Mary Coulter** P (carpenter) came on 13th November address Gortivey

1884 **Minnie Gamble** P (farmer) **James Coulter** P (carpenter) aged 7 in 1886, fees 26s left 1893

1885 **William Coulter** aged 13, P (carpenter) came from Bready Sch aged 13, fees 4d left 1886 **James Millar** P (labourer) lived at Meenaghhill, Bready fees 5s 2d left

1887

1886 **Samuel Coulter** P (carpenter) aged 8 in 1888, fees 6s left 1894 – by 1901 Coulters were in Cloughboy, Co Tyrone

1888 **Frank Sweeny** RC (labourer) **Maggie Sweeny** RC Maggie had attended Killmallaght Sch before coming to Bready School on 30th November 1886 aged 7 when the family moved to Coolmaghery.

1892 **Alexander Thompson** P (blacksmith) aged 6, left 1895

1899 **Robert McIvor** aged 12, P (farmer) came from Bready Sch into 6th Grade, left 1900

1901 **Jack Irvine** P (spirit merchant)

Gortmonley

1881 **William A Clements** (farmer) C of I aged 5 in 1882, fees 28s 1d left 1888 **Charlotte Clements** C of I (farmer)

1887 **Jacob Clements** C of I (farmer) in 1890 aged 6, left 1897 aged 14

1890 **John J Clements** C of I (farmer) – not in census

1896 **Samuel Clements** C of I (farmer) - aged 8 in 1898, left 1903 A Samuel (Mc) Clements from Gortmonley went to Bready Sch on 17th October 1904 aged 14-same person ?

1903 **James Haslett** P (farmer)

Tagherina

1869 **Cassie McClure** P (farmer) aged 7 in 1877? Fees 19s 0 ½ d left 28th May 1881

1873 **James Jeffrey** P (farmer) aged 8, came from Killymallaght Sch fees 12s 10d left 5th April 1879 **James McClure** aged 8, P (farmer) came from Killymallaght Sch fees 5s left 1878 **Jane McClure** P (farmer) aged 7, came from Killymallaght Sch on 31st July fees 36s

1876 **William McClure** aged 7, P (farmer) came from Killymallaght Sch fees 27s 2d left 1881 **William J Jeffrey** P (farmer) aged 6 in 1878, fees 49s 11d left 1884

1877 **Alex Jeffrey** P (farmer) aged 7 in 1879, fees 30s 4d left 1885

1879 **Maggie Mc Clure** P (farmer) **Sarah I Jeffrey** P (farmer)

1882 **Samuel Jeffrey** P (farmer) aged 6 in 1884, fees 147s 9d left 1891 also in 1892 rolls aged 14 and left 1893

1887 **Thomas Jeffrey** P (farmer) aged 7 in 1889, fees 2s left 1893

Glenderowen? Glenderone

1871 **John Adair** RC (widow) aged 12

1873 **Bella Adair** RC (widow)

1898 **Samuel Wilson** P (farmer) aged 16? came from Greerstown Sch into 6th Grade left 1900 **David Wilson** aged 9, P (farmer) came from Greerstown Sch left 1900

1906 **William J Smalls** RC (farmer)

Londonderry

1869 **Maggie Doherty** RC (cow dealer)

Cassie Parker C of I **Annie Parker** C of I came from Bishop Street Sch – no date given

Cloghogle Co Tyrone

1884 **James Millar** P (labourer) did he go to Bready Sch aged 4 in 6th June 1882 – a foundling?

1888 **William J Henderson** aged 11, P (car driver) came from Bready Sch fees 18s 9d left 1891 **Robert Henderson** aged 7, P (car driver) came from Bready Sch – a Robert and William Henderson attended Bready in 1885/6 fees 16s left 1891

Tamneymore

1874 **James Gillespie** RC aged 8, (labourer) came from Waterside Male Sch on 29th July and left in December 1874

1894 **David Moran** RC aged 10, (mason) came from St Columb's Male **Sch Daniel**

Moran RC (mason) aged 10, came on 8th Oct from St Columb's Male Sch into 4th Grade and left 29th Dec 1894

Bogagh

1884 **Hugh Harley** RC aged 8 (labourer) fees 6s left 1889 **Bella Harley** RC (labourer) came from Greerstown Sch

Drumcorkin

1892 **William Parkhill** RC (labourer) aged 6 left 1898

Castlemellon, Co Tyrone

Rebecca Colhoun came from Castlemellon Sch

Glendermott

1874 **Ellen J Gallagher** RC aged 7, left 18th Dec 1875

Ballyartan

1878 **Jane Devine** RC (farmer) aged 11, fees 50s 3d left 1883

Pupils 1911 -22

Some names are taken from Roll Books in the April-June period of the years shown, although a few are from October to December as months are missing from some Roll Books. Those attending school in a given year may vary therefore as pupils left or were enrolled at a later date. Information has also been included from the school's Daily Report Book. I have also attempted to show where pupils lived from 1911 census or other sources when addresses were no longer included in rolls.

Report Books recorded that there were 84 pupils in 1914 By 1919 there were 86 pupils 1920 89 pupils 1921 85 pupils and 1922 86 pupils.

Glenderowen

1912 **William I Smalls** RC (farmer) aged 13, came from Greerstown Sch (he was already registered in 1906) left 29th June 1912

1915 **Joseph Campbell** P (farmer) left 21st May 1915

Magheracannon

1912 **Patrick Lynch** RC (orphan) aged 8, left 7th Sept 1912

1916 **Eddie Devlin** aged 7, RC (labourer) came from Waterside Boys Sch left 30th June 1922

1918 **Sara Flynn** RC **Greta Flynn** RC 4th year

1920 **Georgina Flynn** RC

1921 **John McCloskey** RC (labourer) left 13th April 1929

Coolmaghery Co Tyrone

1913 **Robert McGonagle** P (labourer) aged 8, came from Faughanvale Sch into 2nd yr left 22nd Jan 1916 **Mike Gallagher** RC (labourer) **Alex Olphert** P aged 4, (labourer) left 11th Nov 1916 **Tom Olphert** P (labourer) aged 6, left 11th Nov 1916

1915 **James McGonagle** aged 9 P (labourer) came from Faughanvale Sch left 22nd Jan 1916

1916 **John Lynch** RC (labourer) aged 6 left 30th June 1922

1917 **Henreitta (Nettie) McLaughlin** P (chemist) went to Bready Sch 11 Oct 1920

1918 **Annie McLaughlin** P (2nd year) (chemist) went to Bready 11 Oct 1920 **James McLaughlin** P (chemist) –Coolmaghery House **John McLaughlin** P (chemist) aged 5, left 2nd Oct 1920

1919 **Michael Burns** RC (orphan) came from Enagh Lough NS aged 12, left 1st Nov 1919

1921 **John Lynch** RC (labourer) aged 6, left 10th June 1922

Newbuildings

1911 **James Devlin** RC (labourer) left 8th Nov 1913

1914 **Sam Browne** RC (labourer) left 14th Dec 1914? -maybe 1924 **Tom Gillespie** RC (labourer) aged 4, left 31st May 1924

1915 **Robert Walker** P (merchant) age 6, from a Private School Waterside left 11th Sept 1920

1919 **David Wilkinson** RC (ex soldier) aged 4, left 5th June 1926 **Peter Wilkinson** RC (ex soldier) aged 4, left 5th June 1926

1920 **Dorothy Donnell** C of I (warder) **Martha Wilson** P came from Bennet St Sch (born in 1915)

1922 **Mary (May) Smallwoods** – may have come from Tamneymore

Dunhugh-also Dunhue

1915 **Leslie Hartford** C of I aged 5, (traveller) left 18th Oct 1915

1918 **James Osbourne** P came from Clooney Trc Sch aged 10, left 17th Nov 1923 **Thomas (Tom) Osborne** P came from Clooney Trc Sch aged 7, left 15th May 1923 **Tillie McCan** C of I

1918 **Maggie Byers** P (3rdYear) **Annie Byres** P (3rdyear) **Jeannie McCan** P (5th year) **Anna McCan** P 2nd Year

1919 **Andrew Curran** RC **Lily Houston** P

1921 **May Hegarty** P **Robert (Bob) Osbourne** P aged 6, left 17th Nov 1923

Drumcorkin

1916 **James McCorkell** Cof I (labourer) aged 7, left 19th June 1920 **Maggie McCorkell** C of I (labourer)

1918 **Rebecca (Becky) McCorkell** C of I (labourer) 4th year **Catherine Ann (Katie) Mc Corkell** C of I (labourer)

Gortinure

1911 **John Crumley** RC (farmer)

1917 **Edward J Lynch** (shipyard worker) came from Killea Sch left 11th Nov 1922 **Samuel R Kyle** P aged 9, (French polisher) left 5th Aug 1917 **William J Kyle** P (French polisher) aged 10, left 5th Aug 1917 **John Orr** M-also given as C of I (French polisher) left 3rd Aug 1918

1918 **Aileen Hyndman** P (6th year) (farmer)

1919 **Andrew Curran** RC (labourer) left 23rd May 1920

1920 **Sam J Jackson** P left 22nd Oct 1921

Half Mile Hill

1917 (6th Year) **Catherine J (Cassie) Collins** RC

Dam Row. Newbuildings Village

1911 **Sara McGrory** RC

1915 **Peggy Gallagher** RC

1916 **Irene McLaughlin** P **John J Cassidy** aged 6, (soldier) –may be called James or Jim left 14th June 1924 **Nan Cassidy** RC (fowl dealer)-the Cassidy family came to live in Dam Row after 1914-18 war from Scotland-their father Charlie had been an ambulance driver in the Army Medical Core **John McGrory** RC (labourer) aged 6, left 22nd Sept 1923

1918 (6th Year) **Kathleen Moorhead** P **John Mc Laughlin** P **Rosanna Phillips** RC (labourer) **Agnes Phillips** RC

1919 **Edward Phillips** RC aged 4, came on 29th Sept left 7th April 1927 – another Eddie Phillips aged 4 came on 3rd June and left on 2nd May 1926 **Annie Monteith** P **Charles (Charlie) Cassidy** RC (fowl dealer) left 10th Sept 1927

1920 **Maud Monteith** P

1922 **Alec Kelly**, RC (labourer) left 18th Jan 1930

Magheramason Co Tyrone

1913 **Bertie McNeely** P (farmer) aged 6, left 1st Nov 1919

1914 **James Allen McLaughlin** P (chemist) left 8th May 1920 **Joseph (Josie) Clements** P (farmer) aged 6, left 13th Aug 1921

1916 **Bernard Hassan** RC age 5, (blacksmith) left 3rd Oct 1917

1917 **Mollie McNeely** P (farmer)

1918 **Margaret Mc Neely** P (farmer) 3rd year **Willie McNeely** P (farmer) 6th year **Agnes Gamble** P (farmer) **Willie Gamble** P (farmer) aged 5 left on 23rd Sept 1922 **Greta Gamble** P (farmer)

1920 **Mamie Gamble** P (farmer)

1921 **Jack (John) Mc Neely** P (farmer) left 13th Sept 1930

1922 **Jeannie Gamble** P (farmer)

Clampernow

1912 **Ernest Smyth** P (widow) –also given as farmer? Left 5th Aug 1917

1918 **Edith Walker** P (labourer) **Maud Walker** P (labourer) **Caroline A Walker** P (labourer) **Robert N Walker** P (4th year) **William Walker** P (William is aged 5 at Bready with Edith aged 10 and Maud Walker aged 11 on 7th June 1920 – they are recorded as living in Magheramason –had left Rossnagalliagh on 5th June 1920 **Evelyn Walker** P (labourer) into 5th year **Margaret Walker** P into 5th year (labourer)

Rossnagalliagh

1911 **Bobbie Gillespie** RC (labourer) left 19th Jan 1918 **Sarah Gillespie** RC came from Greerstown Sch on 11th September she was 13 years old

1912 **James Moyne** RC (widow) left 16th Oct 1915

1914 **Daniel Moyne** RC (widow) **Willie Browne** RC (labourer) aged 7, left 29th April 1922

1918 **Elizabeth (Lily) Gillespie** RC **Margaret Gillespie** RC -the Gillespies may have moved from Warbleshinney to live at Tully Bridge, later the home of the McCloskeys

1919 **Thomas Gillespie** RC (labourer) left 17th Sept 1927

1921 **James Devine** RC (ploughman) left 30th July 1932

Hillhead

1913 **Jim Toland** RC (labourer) aged 7, left 3rd Aug 1918

1916 **Lily (Llizzie) Browne** RC

1916 **Daniel Toland** aged 8, RC (labourer) also given as surfaceman, came from Faughanvale Sch - address in 1916 is Dunhue - in rolls Dan Toland is aged 11 in 1918 is in 3rd year-left 30th June 1921

1918 **Sam Browne** RC (labourer) - Sam left to go to work in 1927-he later lived at Phillip St, Bolies and Foyle Crescent **William Brown** RC (labourer) 4th year **Mary (May) Toland** 2nd Year **Agnes Brown** RC 5th year (labourer)

1919 **Bernard Toland** RC aged 5, left 3rd July 1929

Ballyorr

1916 **Michael Mellon** RC (carpenter) left 13th Oct 1923

1917 **Annie Mellon** RC (carpenter) 3rd year

1918 **Susie Mellon** RC (carpenter) 4th year **Nellie Mellon** RC (carpenter) **Lily (or Lizzie) Mellon** RC (carpenter) the Mellons lived in the house beside the Chapel **John McCloskey** RC (cattle dealer) aged 6, left 30th April 1927

1919 **Michael Burns** RC **James Mellon** RC (carpenter) left 7th June 1920

1921 **Frank McCloskey** RC (horse dealer) aged 5, left 13th April 1929

1922 **Cornelius McCloskey** RC (dealer) left 30th Jan 1932

Primity

1913 **John Gallagher** RC (labourer) aged 9, left 20th May 1916

1914 **Joseph (Joe) Henry** C of I – also given as P (railroad labourer) came from Clooney Sch age 8, in 1911 census Joe is 10 left 20th Nov 1915 **David Henry** P (labourer) aged 10, came from Clooney Sch left 20th Nov 1915 **John Henry** P (labourer) aged 6, left 19th Oct 1918-another John Henry in 1915 aged 5, P (labourer) from Newbuildings left 20th Nov 1915

1915 **Stephen Henry** P (labourer) aged 4 left 20th Nov 1915 **Tom Gallagher** RC (labourer) aged 6 left 30th June 1922

1916 **Michael Gallagher** aged 8, RC (labourer) left 20th May 1916 **Bridget Gillespie** (5th year) RC **Richard Henry** P (labourer) left 19th Oct 1918 **Jim Gallagher** RC (labourer) aged 4, left 20th May 1916 **Jack McCorkell** P (farmer) aged 4, left 20th July 1924

1918 **Rose Hamilton** RC (milk deliverer) **Jeanie McCorkell** P (farmer)

1919 **Hugh Hamilton** RC (milk deliverer) came from Rosemount Boys Sch aged 7, left 25th Sept 1926 **John Hamilton** RC (milk deliverer) came from Rosemount Boys Sch aged 9, into 3rd year, left 21st June 1924 **Maggie Hamilton** (3[rd]Year) RC (milk deliverer) **Bridget (Bridie) Hamilton** (3[rd]year) RC (milk deliverer) 1921 **Kathleen Hamilton** RC (milk deliverer) **Ada McCorkell** P (farmer)

1921 **David McCorkell** P (widow) aged 5, left 30th July 1927

Gortin

1912 **Thomas John Olphert** P aged 6 (labourer)

1913 **Harry Barr** P (labourer) aged 9, came from Mountcastle Sch left 30th May 1914 **Willie McGinnis** P (labourer) **John Devlin** RC (labourer) aged 7, left 27th Sept 1919

1914 **Robert J Moore** C of I aged 10, (labourer) came from Killymallaght Sch left 30th Sept 1916 **Charles Moore** aged 6, C of I (labourer) came from Killymallaght Sch into Infants left 12th May 1917

1915 **Leo Mullan** aged 8, (labourer) came from Mullaghabuoy Sch into 2nd yr left 7th Nov 1915

1916 **John Townsley** P (ploughman) -1911 census John is living in Craigtown, came from Killymallaght Sch aged 9, left 2nd June 1917 **Charles Hone** RC (milk server) from Killymallaght Sch – in 1911 census address is Tirkeveney-aged 6, left 16th May 1925

1918 **James Hone** RC (milk server) aged 6, left 30th June 1927

1919 **John Kelly** RC (labourer) left 24th Nov 1928

1920 **William (Willie) J Lynch** RC (labourer) came from Bready Sch (infants) left 11th Nov 1922 **Tom P Hone** RC (milkman) **Alexander Kelly** RC

1922 **Tom P Hone** RC (milkman) aged 6 left 22nd Sept 1928 **George Lynch** RC (labourer) aged 7 left 11th Nov 1922

Quay Lane

1914 **Thomas (Tom) Gillespie** RC (labourer) address also Kittybane

1921 **Grace Kilgore** (may be known as Devine)

1917 **John Lynch** RC

1918 **Sara Lynch,**(3rd year)RC **Maggie Lynch** RC **Bridget Gillespie** RC (4th year) **Elizabeth Jane (Lizzie?) Toland** RC (surfaceman) **Kathleen Mc Clements** 4th year

1919 **Patrick Gillespie** RC (surfaceman) left 30th June 1928

1920 **Kathleen Lynch** RC 3 rd Year **Eddie Lynch** RC

1921 **Sam Lynch** RC **George Lynch** RC

Donemana/Dunamanagh Road

1916 **Bella Gillespie** RC

1918 **Bridget Mc Ginley** RC **Maggie Gillespie** RC 5th year

 1919 **Dan Mc Ginley** RC (labourer) left 4th Oct 1919 **Annie Mc Ginley** RC **Tillie McGinley** RC **Matilda McGinley** RC (not same person)

1922 **Agnes O' Neill** RC

Lower Tully

1911 **Lizzie Lynch** (labourer) came from St Columb's Female Sch Waterside on 10th July, she was 9 years old and went into 1st year

1913 **Willie Kincaid** aged 12, P (labourer) came from Bridge End Sch Co Tyrone left 16th May 1914 **David Kincaid** aged 9, P (labourer) came from Bridge End Sch Co Tyrone left 16th May 1914

1915 **George Clements** M (farmer) left 18th May 1923

1917 **Alex Clements** M (farmer) aged 6 left 2nd Feb 1924

1918 **Maud Clements** M (farmer) 5th year **Mary J Clements** M (farmer)

1920 **Annie Clements** M (shown as P) (farmer)

Warbleshinney

1918 **Elizabeth (Lily) Gillespie** RC **Margaret Gillespie** RC 5th Year

Waterside

1913 **Samuel Haire** P (coach builder) aged 12, from King St Waterside left 31st March 1917

1914 **Joe Haire** aged 7 P (coachbuilder) came from Ebrington Sch into 1st year left 13th April 1918

1915 **Joseph Noble** aged 12, C of I (labourer) came from Clooney Sch into 3rd year left 25th Sept 1915

Cullion

1912 **William J MCDowell** RC (railway ganger) aged 6, left 24th Oct 1914

Gortmonley

1918 **Kath (Kathleen?) McClements** RC 4th year – also Kittybane

Newbuildings Street

1914 **Willie O'Brien** C of I - also given as P - (labourer) aged 6, left 13th Aug 1921

1918 **Fannie O'Brien** C of I (labourer) into 2nd Grade

1922 **Dorothy Mills** C of I

Prehen

1911 **Robert Burke** P (labourer) aged 7, left 6th May 1916

1915 **Willie Porter** C of I (labourer) aged 10, left 10th Nov 1917

Pupils 1923-34

In 1923 there were 87 pupils. On 23rd September 1924 Mr Donaghey, school inspector, reported 64 present In 1929 there were 43 pupils; 1930-60 pupils 1931- 56 pupils; 1932 -64 pupils; 1933 -63 pupils

Dunhugh

1926 **Willie Mclaughlin** RC (postman) came from St Columb's Girls Sch aged 7, left on 17th Jan 1931 **Harry McLaughlin** RC (postman) came from St Columb's Sch aged 9, left on 17th Jan 1931 – Willy and Harry are recorded as having come from the Girls School **Robert McLaughlin** RC (postman) came from St Columb's Boys Sch aged 12, left on 30th April 1927 **Eileen McLaughlin** RC (postman) came from St Eugene's Girls Sch aged 11, went into 3rd grade, left within 2 months, readmitted 3 months later, struck off in 1927 back in January 1930 and left one month later to go to Lone Moor Road Sch – McLaughlin's address also Primity

1928 **Brendan McLaughlin** RC (postman) aged 5, left 17th Jan 1931

Primity

1927 **Mary Gillespie** RC (ex-soldier) born in 1921-on 1 st April 1930 went to Long Tower Sch but returned on 6th September 1930 Left school on 30th May 1936 to go to work

Station Road –Primity

1925 **Robert J (Bertie) King RC** (railway porter) aged 7, lived in the Station house came from Waterside Boys Sch, left 4th June 1932 **Willy McGinley** (3rd year) (tinsmith) the McGinley family had lived in a caravan on the Old Station Road-left 2nd May 1931

1929 Tilly McGinley (4th year) (tinsmith) **Lawrence King** RC (railway porter) aged 5, came 21st Oct and left on 13th July 1935

Victoria Bridge Co Tyrone

1930 **Jess Mary Teresa Doran** RC (farmer) came from Liscreenaghan Sch aged 9, left 9th May 1931 to go to Holywood Co Down **Brigid (Bridie) Doran** RC (farmer) came from Liscreenaghan Sch aged 8, left 6th Dec 1932 to go to Holywood Co Down

Magheracannon

1926 **Nellie Madden** P (farm worker) came from Carnmoney Sch Co Donegal aged 11, left 30th July 1927

Coolmaghery Co Tyrone

1924 **William A McLaughlin** P (chemist)

1930 **John Murphy** RC (labourer) came from Cloughcor Sch aged 9, address also given as Clampernow

1931 **William A Leckey** P (widow) came from Bready Sch aged 9 on 7th December into Infants, left 27th February 1931 **Thomas Thompson** C of I **Mary J Leckey** C of I (widow) came from Bready Sch into infant class, left on 27th Feb1932 to go to Grange Sch Strabane **Marion Leckey** C of I

1933 **Rena Curry** C of I (labourer) born 1920, came from Earlsgift Sch Donemana into 5th year on 31st January 1933 left on 11th Feb 1933

Clampernow /Upper Tully

1923 James Falconer P (labourer) came from Sandville Sch left on 17th March 1930

1925 **John Bailey** P (farmer) came from Blackfoot Co Tyrone into 3rd Grade left 17th July 1926

1926 **Sarah Falconer** P (labourer)-Sarah was born in 1919, left on 11th November

1933 **Annie Bailey** P (father dead) -born in 1921, left 17th Sept 1927

1928 **Jeanie Falconer** P (labourer) born in 1922, left to go to Killymallaght Sch on 11 th November 1930

1929 **Isobel Henry** C of I (labourer) born 1922, left on 12th Sept 1936 to go to work **Joe Henry** C of I (labourer) aged 9, came from Burnfoot Sch and left on 6th Oct 1934

1930 **Willie Falconer** P (labourer) left 11th Nov 1933 **Iris Falconer** P (labourer) **Sam Mitchell** P (labourer) came from Killymallaght Sch aged 12, left 19th Nov 1932 **Kathleen Mitchell** P (labourer) came from Killymallaght Sch aged 9, left 19th November 1932

1931 **James Norman Dalzell** C of I (printer) came from Clooney Primary Sch on 7th September into 1st Grade, left 17th September 1932

1932 **Margaret Mackey** P (carpenter) born 1923, came on 10th Oct 1932 from Killymallaght Sch into 3rd year, left on 25th Aug 1933 **Marion Mackey** P (carpenter) born 1925, came from Killymallaght Sch on 10th Oct 1932 into 1st year, left on 25th August 1933 **Mary M Dalzell** C of I (printer) date of birth 1925, left on 17th Sept 1932 to go to Derry **John Mackey** P (carpenter) left on 25th August 1933

1933 **Jeannie W J Henry** C of I (labourer) left on 4th Sept 1937 **Joseph Henry** C of I

1934 **William J McGavigan** RC (labourer) left on 14th September 1935 **Andrew McGavigan** RC (labourer) from Cloghcor Sch- the McGavigan boys may have come from Burndennet **Gretta Mackay** P 2nd year

1934 **Margaret Evelyn A Ferguson** P (motor driver) came on 1st Oct 1934 and left on 12th Oct 1937 to go to London

Gortin

1928 **Francis Hone** RC (milkman) into infants, left 7th April 1930

1929 **John Connor** RC (labourer at Gortin Hall) came from Enagh Sch on 6th May, aged 9, and left on 9th September 1929 **Neil Connor** RC (labourer) came from Enagh Sch aged 5 on 21st May, and left on 9th September **Maggie Hone** RC (milk man) 4th year

1933 **Edward Hone** RC   (milkman)

Prehen

1931 **Margaret Callan** RC born 1920, in 2nd year (farmer) left on 22nd Sept 1934 **Mary Callan** RC born 1918, in 3rd year (farmer) left on 3rd Dec 1932 – Callans came from Waterside Girls Sch- family lived at Brick Kilns

1932 **Ruth Campbell** (traveller) C of I born 1928came on 1st July 1932 and left on 10th Dec 1932 **Joan Campbel** (traveller) C of I born 1927 came from Greerstown Sch on 12th Sept 1932 left 10th Dec 1932

Quay Lane (built by local farmer, John McEleney, demolished around 1964)

1931 **John Gillespie** RC

Rossnagalliagh

1925 **Anthony Devine** RC (labourer) aged 5, left 1st June 1934

1926 **John Devine** RC (labourer) aged 4,   left 7th Dec 1935 – went to Eglinton- Devine's may later have lived at Quay Lane **John McColgan** RC (merchant) left 25th Aug 1933 **James (Jim) McColgan** RC (merchant) aged 3 yrs 8mths, left 25th Aug 1933

1928 **Thomas (Tom) Devine** RC left on 7th December 1935 to go to Eglinton

1929 **Mary King** RC - later of Prehen

1933 **William Gardener** P (labourer) came from Drumbeg Co Donegal : **Robert Alexander Gardener** P (labourer) came from Drumbeg Co Donegal – Robert went to Bready Sch on 2nd July 1936 aged 12 **Margaret Gardiner** P (yardman) came from Drumbeg Sch 0n 11th May 1933 into 2nd year and went to Bready Sch 4nd July 1936 aged 13 **Francis Gardiner** P (labourer) never at school before, went to Bready Sch 2nd July 1936 **Phoebe Gardiner** P (yardman/labourer) came on 20th Nov 1933 went to Bready Sch on 4nd July 1936

1934 **Sarah (Sara) Lyttle Gardiner** (6th year) P (labourer) born 1921 came from Drumbeg Sch Co Donegal on 11th May 1933 into 5th year left on 31st Dec 1935

Hillhead, Rossnagalliagh

1928 **Terence Browne** RC (farmer) left 25th Nov 1937

1933 **James Toland** RC

Golf Links , Prehen

1926 **Eileen Gertrude Bull** C of I (caretaker) – lived in Golf Club house-Eileen was born in 1920 **John Bull** C of I (caretaker) aged 7, left 31st Aug 1926

1928 **Ellen Brown** C of I (greenkeeper in Rosemount Bowling Green, Brook Park) born in 1921, Brownes lived in a house on the Knox estate.left on 14th September 1935 to go to work

1929 **Mabel (Mamie) Brown (Browne)** C of I (greenkeeper) born 1923-left on 4th September 1937 to go to work

1932 **Sarah Brown** C of I (greenkeeper) left 1938

1934 **Alexander (Lexie) Brown** C of I (green keeper) Lexie is registered as living at Ballyorr

Burndennet, Co Tyrone

1929 **Angela McColgan** RC (merchant) born 1924, left 14th December 1935 to go to Pump St Prep Sch. 1933 **Margaret McColgan** RC (merchant) came on 1st May 1933 left on 14th Dec 1935 to go to Pump St Prep Sch L'Derry

1934 **Samuel P McColgan** RC (merchant) -McColgan's children of the Principal

Dam Row Newbuildings Village

1923 **George Phillips** RC (labourer) aged 5, left 7th April 1927

1925 **Rose Phillips** RC (labourer) born in 1920 - was this Rosanna - left to go to work 1st June 1934

1927 **Mary Kelly**, RC (labourer) she was born in 1920, left 3rd February 1934 to go to work **Kathleen Kerr** RC (labourer) born in 1922, left in 24th August 1936 to go to work

1928 Mabel Monteith P (docker) born 1923, left on 6th November 1937 to go to work **Jeanie Phillips** RC (docker) born in 1923, left on 25th March 1937 to go to work **Patrick Kelly** RC (dock labourer) aged 5, left on 27th Feb 1937

1929 Maud Monteith P (dock labourer) **Violet Monteith** P (2nd Year) (dock labourer) **Jeannie Monteith** P (dock labourer)

1930 Maggie Kelly RC (labourer) born 1925, left on 22nd April 1939 to go to work in a factory **Susan Phillips** RC born 1925, left 8th Sept 1939 to go to work **Sean Ferry** RC **Maureen Ferry** RC (labourer/ex-miner in Scotland) left on 12 April 1941

1931 Myrtle Goodwin P (soldier) left on 26th Feb 1938 to go to Carlisle Road Sch readmitted 12th April 1938 left 20th Jan 1939 to go to Greerstown Sch readmitted on 15th March 1939 left on 27th Feb 1942 (may also be known as Monteith) **Annie Kelly** RC (dock labourer) left on 18th July 1932 **Margaret Kerr** RC (ex-soldier) left on 20th May 1937

1933 Patrick (Patsy?) Kerr RC left to go to work 31st May 1941

1934 Maud Phillips RC (dock labourer) left on 31 st Oct 1942 to go to work

Newbuildings Street (main Londonderry to Strabane Road now Victoria Road)

1923 Charles Donnell RC (labourer) the Donnell's name was at times written as O'Donnell) left 11th June 1932 **Dan or Dannie Gillespie** RC (surfaceman) aged 5, left 9th April 1932

1924 Edward Hamilton RC (milkman)-address Primity – left 29th June 1929

1925 Francis Donnell RC (labourer) aged 5, left 27th Jan 1934

1927 Hugh Gillespie RC (labourer) aged 5, also given as surfaceman, left 9th Feb 1935 **Margaret Donnell** RC (labourer) left 8th June 1934

1930 John Donnell RC (labourer) **Rita Donnell** RC (labourer) **Eileen Donnell** RC (labourer) **James Hamilton** RC

1934 Walter Collins C of I – lived in tin houses opposite Post Office **Sara J Angela Donnell** RC (labourer) came on 27th Aug 1934 and left on 8th Jan 1944 to go to work. They may have lived at Quay Lane

Newbuildings

1923 **Willie Wilkinson** RC (ex soldier) left 10th July 1926 later lived in Alberta, Canada

1924 **John James Goligher** P (labourer) left 2nd May 1925

1925 **Martha Wilson** P (labourer) came from Bennet St Mixed Sch aged 10 went into to 1st Grade, left 30th June 1927 **Samuel Wilson** P (labourer) aged 9, came from Bennet St Sch, left on 30th June 1927 **Elizabeth Mullan** RC (grandmother) came from Magheracotton, Co Tyrone aged 11, went into 1st Grade, left 8th May 1926

1927 **Michael Brown** RC (labourer) aged 8, came from Glendermott Sch left 6th Nov 1926 **Robert Burke** P (labourer) left 31st March 1926 **William Wilson** P (labourer) aged 6, came from Rosemount Sch left 30th June 1927 **Agnes Browne** RC (labourer) came from Glendermott Sch aged 12 into 1st Grade, left 8th Nov 1926 **Margaret Browne** RC (labourer) came from Glendermott School aged 10 into 1st Grade, left on 8th November 1926 **Henry (Harry) King** RC (carpenter) left 13th May 1935 **Elizabeth Ferris** RC (farm worker) was born in 1915, left 30th April 1927

1929 **Sheena Quigg** RC (grocer) came from Faughan Bridge Sch aged 7, left on 2nd Dec 1931 **Mildred (Millie) Orr** M

1930 **Anthony Maguire** RC (labourer) came from Christian Bros Sch Armagh aged 10 **Lawrence Maguire** RC (labourer) came from Christian Bros Sch Armagh aged 8 **Joseph Maguire** RC (labourer) came from Christian Bros Sch Armagh aged 13 **Rita Maguire** RC (labourer) born 1924, left on 31st March 1931 to go to Armagh **Eileen Donnell** P (warder) came from Legfordrum Sch, Co Tyrone aged 7, left on 23rd March 1934 to go to Waterside **Iris Jackson** P **Dorothy Donnell** P **Reginald C Kelso** P (traveller) **Margaret Gillespie James Kerr** RC (carpenter) aged 5, left 24th Feb 1931

1931 **William Lecky** came on 27th March

1933 **Mary Kerr** RC (itinerant labourer) came from Clog Newry on 13th Feb 1933 into Infants, left on 4th June 1934

1934 **Dorothy Donald** P (warder) came from Killymallaght Sch aged 7, left 23 rd March 1934

Magheramason Co Tyrone

1924 **Andrew McNeely** P (farmer) left 19th July 1930 **Charles A Mills** P – was this Lexie Mills? Left 30th July 1932 **William A McLaughlin** P (chemist) aged 6, left 28th March 1925

1926 **Robin McNeely** P (farmer) aged 6, left 30th June 1932

1928 **Martha Kelly** P (labourer) born in 1920, left to go to Bready Sch on 22 nd Sept 1928 **Sam McNeely** P (farmer) came on 30th April, left 6th July 1935 to go to Foyle College

1929 **Rosemary D Eakin** P (farmer) born 1921, left on 31 st December 1931 to go to Londonderry High School

1935 **Susan Kelly** P born 1926 came from Bready Sch on 26th June 1935 into 1st yr, left on 14th Dec 1940

Lower Tully

1923 **William (Billy) Orr Reid** P (flesher) aged 6, from Waterside Sch left 30th July 1927

1924 **Andrew McGarrigle** P (labourer) aged 13, came from Killymallaght Sch into 3rd year, left 30th Sept 1925

1925 **Maurice Reid** P (flesher) aged 6, left 21st March 1931

1927 **George Irwin Reid** P (flesher) left 21st March 1931 later lived in Australia

1929 **Leonard Reid** P (farmer) aged 5, left 21st March 1931

Myrtle Reid P (flesher) not in rolls - but in 1931 photograph

Drumcorkin

1933 **James Rutherford** P left on 27th April 1935

1934 **Alfred Rutherford** P (labourer) went to Greerstown 27th April 1935 – a Alfred Rutherford P (labourer) had come from Greerstown and was living in Primity/ McCorkell's Brae in 1941 (same boy?)

Ballyorr

1927 **William Mellon** RC (carpenter)

1929 **Cassie Mellon** RC (6th year) **Lily Mellon** RC 3rd year (carpenter)

Dunhugh

1930 **Margaret (Maggie) E Crumley** RC (farmer) left on 13th April 1931

1931 **John Crumley** RC (farmer) **Sarah (Sadie?) Smith** RC (labourer) left on 7th July 1936 to go to Waterside Elementary Sch

1932 **Kathleen Smith** RC (labourer) left on 7th July 1936 to go to Waterside Sch

1934 **Lily (Elizabeth Mary) Smyth** RC (labourer) came on 7th May 1934 and left on 7th July 1934 to go to Waterside Sch

Pupils who attended 1935-1949

The number of pupils who attended in 1935 was 51, 1936-49, 1937-50, 1940-66 1943-71 pupils and 1944 -79 pupils. Mr T J Donaghey, the school attendance officer, visited on 19th June 1944 and recorded only 44 pupils present due to potato digging-the pupils had an official holiday for potato digging in October.

Evacuees from Londonderry came to the school in 1941 and 1942. In October 1941, 45 pupils were recorded by Mr Donaghey plus 6 evacuees, on 6th February 1942- 64 pupils and 2 evacuees, 13th March 1942, 60 pupils plus 1 evacuee and 8th July 1942, 53 pupils and 1 evacuee. By January 1943 57 pupils were recorded but no evacuees.

Burndennet ?

1948 **William B (Billy) Dunne** RC (corn agent) came from Prior Sch Raphoe Co Donegal **Margaret Dunne** - it is thought the Dunnes may have come with the Principal to school

Maghercannon

1949 **Shelia Gillespie** RC (warder/male nurse) came on 29th August 1949, left in 1952 aged 7 to go to Long Tower School **William J Gillespie** RC (warder/male nurse) was to leave in 1952 aged 12

Primity

1939 **James Craig** RC (unemployed) **Julia Craig** RC (unemployed) aged 8, came on 6th Nov 1939 in to 1st year and left on 9th Dec 1939 **Margaret Craig** RC (unemployed) aged 6, left on the same dates as Julia - the Craigs came from St Francis Sch Glasgow

1942 **David Rutherford** P (labourer)-it was noted that he went to hospital on 12th December 1942 but no further information given **Elsie Rutherford** P came on 25th June 1942 from Greerstown Sch and left on 12 June 1944 age 6

1943 **June Rutherford** P (labourer) - the Rutherfords lived at McCorkell's Brae **Kathleen Rutherford?**

1946 **Elizabeth McCrossan** RC (factory) came on 2nd April 1946

Ballyorr

1937 **Nora Toland** RC (labourer) came on 2nd June 1937on 8th Sept 1939 she is struck off the register due to "hospital" but was back in school at some later date as she left in 1945

1939 **Shelia Toland** RC (labourer) came on 25th April 1939 left on 11th July 1942 – recorded as died aged 7

1943 **John Toland** RC (labourer) left school on 19th December 1953 **Colleen McEleney** P (farmer)

Hillhead, Rossnagalliagh

1942 **Lily Toland** RC (labourer) – address in rolls is Ballyorr came on 23rd March 1942 and left in 1945 aged 8

1944 **Daniel Toland** RC (labourer) –also given as David in rolls

Rossnagalliagh

1935 **Peggy Gardiner P** (labourer) **Catherine Gardiner** P (labourer) - address may be Tully came from Earlsgift Sch into 1st yr and left on 3rd Jan 1936 **Patrick Toland** RC (labourer) left on 7th September 1945 **Rose Toland** RC came on 11th March 1935 and left on 11th July 1937

1937 **Kathleen Hamilton** RC (unemployed) came from St Columba's Girls Sch on 28th June 1937 left on 26th Sept 1944 –a niece of Rossnagalliagh Gillespies- tragically killed in a road accident on Prehen Road **Fred Rutherford** P (labourer) left to go to work 16th November 1945 – Fred's father (Willy) is thought to have come from Creeve. Co Donegal and worked on Roulston farm **Violet Boyd** P (labourer) came from Killymallaght Sch (also given as coming from Greerstown Sch) into Infants on 24th May 1937 left on 23rd Sept 1944 **Sadie (Sarah) Boyd** (labourer) came from Killymallaght Sch (also given as Greerstown Sch) on 24th May 1937 left on 14th Jan 1939 to go to work, later lived at Foyle Crescent Rd **James Boyd** P (labourer) came from Greerstown Sch and left Rossnagalliagh to go to work on 9th September 1939 **John Boyd** P (labourer) came from Greerstown Sch left Rossnagalliagh to go to work on 5th December 1942

1939 **Isobel King** RC (gardener) born 1932, came on 5th June 1939 from Waterside Girls Sch into Junior Infants, left 1945 **Theresa King** RC (gardener) came on 5th June 1939 aged 6, left 1945

1940 **Robert Boyd** P (farm labourer) left to go to work on 30th April 1948 – the Boyd family lived opposite Roulstone's farm **Patrick King** RC (gardener) went to Boys School 6th October 1949 – may have been Christian Brothers School **Shelia Toland** RC (labourer) **Alex W Roulston** P (farmer) went to the Model School 18th July 1942 – Alex and William had come from Creeve Co Donegal and attended Monreagh National School Co Donegal before coming to Rossnagalliagh **William McD Roulstone** P (farmer) went to Model School 18th July 1942 **John H Roulston** P (farmer) went to the Model Sch on 18th July 1942 **Maria Rutherford** P (labourer) came on 9th April 1940 left on 24th April 1948 aged 13 **Elsie Rutherford** P (labourer) came on 9th April 1940 left 1945

1941 Evacuee **Colm Gillespie** RC (pict manager?) left to go to St Eugene's Infant School 14th April 1942 **George Logan** P (labourer) **Margaret Lynch** P Evacuee **Harry Hamilton** RC (farm labourer) left 24th May 1941 Evacuee **Hugh Hamilton** RC (farm labourer) left to go to Long Tower School 24th May 1941 **Annie Logan** P (labourer) came on 7th May 1941 from Bready Sch into 2nd year and left 1945 aged 13

1942 **Joseph King** RC left 31st May 1943 **William Kelly** RC (dock labourer) changed residence but not recorded where to **Robert S Logan** P (labourer) left the district to go to Bready on 31st July 1949. In Bready's records he came on 3rd Oct 1949. He lived at Meenagh Hill, Co Tyrone **William McCorkell** C of I left Rossnagalliagh Sch on 3rd March 1949 to go Bready Sch aged 13

1943 **Marion Lynch** P - a Martha Lynch P came on 12th Nov 1943 and left on 25th Dec (Xmas day?) 1943 – was this the same person? **Sarah Logan** –was she known as Cissie? Came on 9th April 1945 and moved to Bready Sch 3rd Oct 1949 age 10 **Colleen Mc Eleney** P (farmer) came on 19th May 1943 and left on 7th Sept 1951 to go to First Derry Sch **John Toland** RC left on 19th December 1953

1944 **David Boyd** P (labourer) **David Roulston** P (farmer) came on 17thApril left on 30th June 1944

1945 **James King** RC (gardener)

1946 Mary Kathleen King RC (gardener) came on 20th May 1946

1947 **Mary Teresa Logan** P (farm worker) (known as Minnie?) who had come on 20th May 1947 and to Bready Sch on 3rd Oct 1949 age 8 The family lived at Meenaghhill Co Tyrone.

1948 **Thomas Logan** P (labourer) left on 23rd September 1949. In Bready Sch records he came on 3rd October 1949 aged 6. The family had moved to Meenaghhill Co Tyrone.

1949 **Anthony King** RC (gardener) left to go to work on 30th September 1950

Dunhugh / Half Mile Hill

1935 **George Smyth** RC (labourer) **Daniel Crumley** RC (farmer) left on 24th June 1944

1936 **Mark Brickland (Buckland)** RC (farmer) came from Waterside Boys Sch **Agnes Brickland (Buckland)** RC (farmer) came from Waterside Sch on 31st March 1936 and left on 6th June 1936 **Phoebe Brickland (Buckland)** RC (farmer) came on 6th April 1936 and left on 6th June 1936 **Bridget Smyth** RC (farm labourer) came on 20th April 1936 and left on 7th Nov 1936 to go to Waterside

1941 **Susan Crumley** RC (farmer) came on 19th Mary 1941 and left 1945 aged 10

1949 **Kathleen Crumley** RC (farmer) came on 4th April 1949 and left on 31st March 1959 to go to work

Golf Links, Prehen

1936 **William Brown** C of I (greenkeeper) left to go to work 30th September 1945

Newbuildings

1935 **Mary Gillespie** RC

1941 Evacuee **John P Lynch** RC (foreman munition factory) from St Eugene's Sch (Babies) left on 19th September 1942 **Patrick Kelly** RC (docker) left district on 27th April 1945

1945 **Eileen Kelly** RC (dock labourer) came on 9th April 1945 and left on 30th June 1945

1946 **John McGinley** RC (timber) - G McLaughlin thought this might have been tinker as his father repaired pots and pans - left district in 6th October 1947

Dam Row, Newbuildings Village

1935 **Ralph Monteith** P (labourer) left on 14th December 1943

1936 **Patrick W Ferry** RC (labourer) left on 26th January 1945 **Sarah Kelly** RC (dock labourer) came on 16th March 1936 and left on 12 Feb 1944 to go to work **Thomas Kerr** RC (labourer) **Sarah Kerr** RC (labourer) came on 25th Aug 1936 and left in 1944 **Jack Monteith** P **Ronald Monteith** P (labourer) went to Greerstown Sch on 11th Jan 1947

1937 **William Kerr** RC (labourer) left to go to work 0n 3rd October 1947

1939 **Elizabeth K Ferry** RC (miner) came on 6th March 1939 left in 1945 **Robert Monteith** P (labourer) went to Greerstown Sch on 11th January 1947

1940 **Olive Margaret Monteith** P (dock labourer) came on 26th April 1940 and left in 1945 aged 9

1941 James Cleary RC (a wandering minstrel-gypsy) came from Christian Bros Sch left 28th March 1942 **Patrick Cleary** RC (wandering minstrel –gypsy) came from

Ballyshannon Sch Co Donegal left 28th March 1942 **Francis Cleary** (wandering minstrel-gypsy) –the family lived in a caravan in the Dams area- Newbuildings which was a temporary address

1942 **Rebecca E-Monteith** P (dock labourer) may have been known as Ruby left 1946

1943 **David Monteith P** (dock labourer) went to Greerstown School on 11th January 1947 –was he also in the rolls as Daniel? Went to Greerstown on same date.

1944 **Samuel Kerr** RC (carpenter) **Charles (Charlie) Cassidy** RC (fisherman)

1945 **Patrick George McLaughlin** RC (ex Royal Air force) **Elizabeth Agnes (Lily) McLaughlin** RC (ex Corporal -Royal Air Force) came 13th Nov 1945

1946 **Rosemary Cassidy** RC (fisherman) came on 13th May 1946 address given as Primity later Foyle Crescent

1948 **Walter Allan Monteith** P (labourer) left on 8th January 1954 **Charlotte Ada McLaughlin** RC (ex RAF) came on 19th Oct 1948 and left on 13th May 1950-unexplained why but she must have returned to Rossnagalliagh as on 30th Sept 1958 she left to go to work

1949 **Peter Cassidy** RC (labourer) –later of Foyle Crescent

Norman Monteith P

John Cassidy, Tony Cassidy (source- G McLaughlin)

Burndennet /Strabane Co Tyrone

1935 **Margaret McColgan** RC (merchant)

1940 **Collette Mc Colgan** RC (merchant/farmer) came on 30th July 1940 from Waterside Girls Sch into Junior Infants and left on 20th June 1944 aged 9 to go to Mt Carmel Prep Sch, Strabane

1942 **Noeleen McColgan** RC (merchant/farmer) came on 4th May 1942 and left on 20th June 1944 to go to Mt Carmel Prep Sch Strabane **Olive McGrory**

1944 **Kathleen McGettigan** RC (farmer) came on 12th June 1944 from Drummeny Strabane into infants and left 1945

Upper Tully

1935 **Robert Ferguson** P (motorman) went to London 12 th Oct 1937 **Susan Kelly** P

1936 **Anthony Bonner** RC (labourer) came from or went to Castlemellon **Margaret Henry** C of I came on 7th April 1936 and left on 4th Sept 1937 to go to Coleraine

1937 **Major James Ferguson** P (motorman)

1941 Evacuee **John Doherty** RC (Merchant Navy) from Shantallow Sch left on 20th Dec 1941 Evacuee **George Doherty** RC from Shantallow Sch left on 20th Dec 1941 **Rosaline Doherty** RC (Merchant Navy) came on 23rd April 1941 and left on 20th Dec 1941 **Kathleen Doherty** RC came from Shantallow into infants on 23rd April 1941 and left on 20th Dec 1941

Tully Bridge nr Rossnagalliagh

1936 **Gerry Browne** RC left to go to work 25th November 1945 **John Brown** RC left in 1945 **William Browne** RC (farmer) left to go to work 30th April 1948 –family later at Foyle Crescent

1946 **Sam Campbell** C of I (labourer) came from Oghill Sch **Annie Campbell** C of I came on 15th Oct 1946 aged 8, from Oghill Elementary Sch into 2nd year **Isobel Campbell** C of I (labourer) came on 15th Oct 1946 into 4th Year aged 7 **John Campbell** C of I (labourer) came from Oghill Sch and went to Killymallaght Sch on 28th August 1948 **Fanny Campbell** C of I (labourer) came on 21st Oct 1946 from Oghill Elementary Sch into Infants **Elizabeth Campbell** C of I (labourer) came on 15th Oct 1946 into 5th year

1948 **Kathleen Campbell** C of I (labourer) came on 12 April 1948 left 13th May 1950 **Violet Campbell** C of I (labourer) came on 12th April 1948 and left on 13th May 1950 **John McCloskey** (taken from C McLaughlin's list)

1949 **Robert Campbell** C of I (labourer) -the Campbell family came from Fawney to Tully Bridge

Lower Tully

1935 **Robert Gardiner** C of I (labourer) came from Earlsgift Sch. On 6th January 1936 Robert went to Bready Sch aged 11 **Catherine Gardiner** C of I (labourer) came from Earls Gift Sch Donemana and on 6th January 1936 went to Bready Sch aged 8

1937 **Elizabeth Falconer** P (labourer) born 1930 came from Killmallaght Sch on 27th April 1937 into 1st year and left in 13th May 1939 - may then have lived in Drumagor

1939 **Patricia McLaughlin** C of I (railway servant) aged 8, came from Glebe Co Tyrone - date in another register came on 20th Feb 1940 into infants left 1944 **Leslie McLaughlin** C of I (porter LMS) came from Glebe Co Tyrone left Rossnagalliagh on 26th August 1944 to go to Model Sch

1940 **George McLaughlin** C of I (railway servant/porter) went to Model Sch on 26th July 1947

1945 **Gilbert Mclaughlin** C of I (ex-soldier/porter)

1947 **Helen McLaughlin** C of I (porter) Helen died perhaps 13 years old-source G McLaughlin

Newbuildings Street (now Victoria Road)

1936 **Rose Gillespie** RC (labourer) came on 18th May 1936 and left in 1944

1939 **Kathleen McCracken** P (signalman) - came from Clandeboyne Co Down. – although Kathleen gives her date of arrival as 1939 in her memories of her school days-the date in the register give her birth as 15th April 1934 and date of arrival as 8th Jan 1940 when she went into 1st year, left 1947 The McCracken family were to return to Clandeboyne Estate in 1958 as the Railway at Newbuildings had closed – Mr McCracken got employment as a game keeper at Clandeboyne. **Rose Cullinane**- also known as Rosemary, RC (publican/merchant) born 1934 - also shown to have started on 6th May 1940 left on 30th Oct 1943 to go to Prep Sch Convent **Albert Leckey** C of I (postman) came from Killymallaght Sch left Rossnagalliaghto go to work on 24th August 1940 **James Leckey** C of I (postman) came from Killymallaght Sch left to go to work 18th March 1944 **David Leckey** C of I (postman) came from Killymallaght Sch left Rossnagalliagh to go to work on 23rd March 1945 **Eva Leckey**

C of I (postman) came from Killymallaght Sch on 31st August – aged 11 into 5th year, left on 28th March 1942 to go to work -also known as the Leckey/Cunningham family-address in register is Primity -may have lived at Foyle Crescent in 1950's

1940 **Helen McCracken** P (signal man) came on 15th April 1940 and left on 24th August 1948 **Mary McCracken** P (signal man) came on 28th Oct 1940 and left in 1945 aged 9 **George Cunningham** C of I (exsoldier/postman) later of Foyle Crescent

1941 **Bridgid (Bridie) Cullinane** RC (publican/merchant) came on 3rd March 1941 aged 5 and left to go to Prep Sch Convent on 30th Oct 1943 **Rosaline Doherty** RC **Kathleen Doherty**

1944 **Bridget Gillespie** RC also known as Bridie? came on 17th April 1944 and left in 1945 **Celine Cullinane** RC (publican/grocer/merchant) came on 17th April 1944 and left 3rd Nov 1949 to go to Boarding Sch **William George Holmes** C of I (labourer) **Robert (Bertie) Cunningham** C of I (postman) left on 30th August 1950 -later of Foyle Crescent

1945 **Richard McCracken** P (signalman in Great Northern Railway)

1946 **Francis (Frankie) McCracken** P (signal man) it was noted he was off school on 7th March 1947 due to whooping cough and on 8th April 1950 he had a road accident and had an operation to put a "plate" into his head but returned to school.

1949 **Robert (Bobbie) Holmes** C of I (labourer)

1945 **Margaret (Pearl) Holmes** C of I (store keeper) came on 19th Feb 1945 and left on 7th Nov 1949

Lorraine Holmes C of I (labourer) (Kathleen Donaghey 'nee Crumley and G McLaughlin)

Gortin

1936 **Stanley McDermott** P (father was described as a day labourer but a Stanley McDermott is also known locally as son of farmer who lived at Gortin Hall) went to Model Sch on 4th September 1937

1937 **James Barnett** C of I (labourer) came from Bready School?

1940 **Emily Jean Lynch** C of I (labourer) came on 8th Jan 1940 and left in 1944 **James Robinson** C of I (labourer) left to go to work 2nd March 1945 - the Robinson children had come from Killymallaght Sch on 4th November **David Robinson** C of I (labourer) **Robert Barnett** C of I (labourer) went to Bready Sch on 8th April 1941 aged 8, his address at Bready was Coolmaghery

1941 Evacuee **Jack McNulty** P (musician) came from Carlisle Road School left on 24th May 1941 **Margaret Lynch** P (labourer) came on 1st Sept 1941 and left in 1944 aged 9 Evacuee **Ivan Bell** C of I (coachman) from Fountain St Londonderry had attended Derry Cathedral Sch (babies) came on 1st September 1941 and left on 31st Sept **Irene Bell** C of I (coach man) from Fountain St had attended Derry Cathederal Sch came on 1st Sept 1941 and left on 30th Sept 1941 **Sara Gillespie** came on 6th May 1941 and left 1945 aged 9

1942 **Joyce Robinson** C of I (labourer)came on 28th April 1942 and left in 1945 **Lavinia (Vina) Robinson** C of I (labourer) left on 23rd April 1945

1943 **Iris Collette** C of I (labourer) left on 22nd March 1947 **Dorothy Collette** C of I left on 3rd Sept 1945

1945 **William J Gillespie** RC (land stewart) **Annie E C B Collette** C of I (labourer) came from Killymallaght Sch into Infants on 6th March 1943 and left on 30th June 1945

1947 **Robert Lynch** C of I (labourer) came in February and left a month later **Iris Isobella Robinson** C of I (labourer) came on 2nd June 1947

1948 **John Robinson** Cof I (labourer)

Eva Robinson-not in rolls therefore unsure of date. Name from a local source

Coolmaghery Co Tyrone

1935 **Adelaide Jones** C of I (gypsy) **Isobel Jones** C of I (gypsy) Isobel came on 7thOct 1935 – there is a question mark about her age which is given as 7 – left on 12th Oct 1935 Adelaide came and left on the same date as Isobel-her age is give as 8 with a question mark **Thurles Jones** C of I (gypsy) **Jocelyn P Kavanagh** C of I (mechanic) left on 25th Jan 1936

1939 **Cecil Ballard** P (gardener) came to Coolmaghery from Fivemiletown Co Tyrone. He left Rossnagalliagh to go to Bready Sch on 13th April 1945 Bready's records indicate he came on 10th April and that his father was a railway worker. He was 12 years of age

1940 **George McLaughlin** P - two G McLaughlins? Other from L Tully in same year **Jack Ballard** P (gardener) went to Bready Sch on 13th April 1945-Bready's records indicate he came on the 10th April and his father was a railway worker. He was 11 years of age

1941 Evacuee **Henry Mercer** (3rd year) lived in Fountain Street, Londonderry and from Derry Cathedral Sch on 1st Sept 1941 and left on 30th Sept **Meta Mercer** C of I (motor driver) into 3rd year-address Fountain Place (may be Fountain Street) came on 1st Sept 1941 from Derry Cathedral Sch and left on 11th Oct 1941 aged 9 **Irene Mercer** C of I (motor driver) into (3rd or 5[th]year) on 1st Sept 1941 **Lily Mercer** C of I came on 1st Sept 1941 from Derry Cathedral Sch and left on 11th Oct 1941

1943 **Desmond Ballard** P (fire watcher) went to Bready aged 7 on 13 th April 1945 although Bready's records show 10th April and father as a railway worker. Rossnagalliagh's records show he lived at Magheramason

Magheramason Co Tyrone

1935 **David Kelly** P (labourer) left on 29th August 1937

1936 **Herbert Joseph Campbell** P (clerk) **William C Campbell** P (clerk) and went to Bready on 15th March 1939

1938 **Elizabeth A Campbell** P (clerk) came on 2nd May 1938 struck off register on 14th Jan 1939-may be due to illness but back on 21st March 1939- left on 8th Sept 1939 destination Derry

1939 **Ethel Campbell** P (clerk) came on 24th March 1939 left on 8th Sept 1939 to go to Derry

Tagherina

1937 **James Campbell** P (unemployed?) went to Clooney Sch on 9th Apr in Bready Sch on 8th May 1939- **Margaret I Campbell** P (unemployed) age 7 came from Killymallaght Sch into Infants (off school due to illness 28th Jan 1939- 21 st March

1939) left on 8th Sept 1939 to go to Derry

Gortmesson Co Tyrone

1942 **Andrew Griffin** RC – he came on 6th October and left on 10th October to live at Campsie **Mary Griffin** RC (labourer) came on 6th Oct 1942 and left on 12 Dec 1942 to go to Waterside

Tamnakerry Co Tyrone

1939 **Maria Olphert** C of I (farmer) came from Bready Sch on 3rd July 1939 aged 13 into 4th year left 6th Sept 1940 aged 14 – Bready Sch records show Maria began school there on 27th September 1932 aged 6

Gortinure

1937 **Rose Malseed** RC (orphan) came from St Mary's Glasgow on 2nd Sept 1937 left to go to Waterside Girls Sch on 26th March 1938 came back 9th April 1942 but returned to Waterside Girls Sch on 19th Dec 1942

1942 **Charles Mullan** RC (fire service) left 17th July 1943 **Margaret M Mullan** RC (labourer) from Greerstown Sch into Infants left on 17th March 1943 to go to Waterside Girls Sch

Donemana /Dunamanagh Road (later Duncastle Road)

1939 **Kathleen G Gillespie** RC (labourer) left in 1945 – address may be Primity

1941 **Kathleen D Gillespie** RC **Harold S Gillespie**, RC

1942 **Margaret G Mullan** RC **Sarah (Sadie?) Gillispie** RC

1944 **John William McNair** C of I (soldier) came from Derry Cathedral Sch **Samuel McNair** C of I (soldier) came from Derry Cathedral School **Sarah McNair** C of I (soldier) came on 5th April 1944 from Derry Cathedral Sch and left 1947 –lived in house nearest the chapel

1945 **William Gillespie** RC (unemployed)

1946 **Patrick (Paddy) Gillespie** RC (labourer) - unfortunately this pupil was drowned in River Foyle near the Fisheries, Newbuildings –local source

Railway Station, Newbuildings

1949 **Robert (Bertie) Crossan** (boilerman)

See 1949 photo not in rolls - **Noleen Crossan** (boilerman)

Quay Lane

1935 Hugh (Hugo) Gillespie RC (labourer) left on 2nd March 1945

1940 **James (Seamus) Gillespie** RC (labourer)

1941 **Dolores Gillespie** RC (labourer) born 1937 – known as Dora or Doreen? came on 13th March 1941 and left 1945

1943 **Daniel Gillespie** RC (labourer) left on 15th April 1955-in rolls also given as David

1945 **Annie Gillespie** RC (labourer) came on 26th March 1945 and left on 30th June 1945

1949 **Brigid Gillespie** RC (orphan) came on 29th August 1949 left on 22nd Dec 1960 to go to work

Angela Donnell aged 13

Phillip Donnell RC (unemployed) left to go to work on 5th July 1947

1947 **Margaret A Gillespie** RC (labourer) came on 10th June 1947 **Elizabeth A Gillespie** RC (labourer) left in 1952 aged 11 –one of these girls may have been called Angela – if so they were twins **Isobel Ashley Gillespie** RC (recorded as an orphan?) came on 1st July 1947 left on 25th March 1958

Kitttybane

1946 **Robert (Bobby) Gillespie** (foreman) left on 22nd December 1960

1948 **Thomas Gillespie** left to go to work 30th September 1958

Londonderry

1941 **Pauline Gillespie** RC (PH Manager?) came on 14th July 1941 address given as Ernest St left on 14th Feb 1942 may have been an evacuee

1942 **Mary Harkin** RC (itinerant) came on 14th Sept 1942 from Rosemount Girls Sch into Infants and left on 5th Dec 1942

1946 **Margaret Ann Moran** RC (labourer) came on 29th Jan 1946 from 15 Duke St Waterside

1940 **Agnes Phillips** RC

1950's

Only a minimum of information was available at PRONI and most roll books are missing altogether for this decade, The date of when some pupils began school therefore is calculated from their age when they first appear in a registrar in the 1960's and some pupils may not be recorded here at all. Some names, addresses and father's occupations were given by past pupils whose names are shown in brackets or beside addresses.

Although the numbers attending are unknown, past pupils indicate that the number attending school was low and a photograph taken in 1958/9 period show only 26 pupils at the school. However the Daily Report Book indicated that between July 1958 and December 1959 there were 36-40 pupils.

After 1955, when Newbuildings Primary School opened, the children remaining at Rossnagalliagh were all Roman Catholic. From this date, therefore, I have not recorded the pupil's religion.

Foyle Crescent was a new social housing estate built in Newbuildings in mid 1950's.

Primity

1950 **Sara Rutherford** C of I (orphan) came on 1st May 1950 from Greerstown Sch

Dam Row

1948/51 **James Phillips** RC (Margaret Boyd)

1950 **Francis Cassidy** RC (fisherman), (Margaret Boyd, G McLaughlin and S Browne) **Rosemary McLaughlin** RC (telephone operator) came on 30th June 1950 and left on 30th June 1960

1951 **Patrick (Patsy) Kelly** RC (bricklayer) (J Mitchell)

1954 **Eileen McLaughlin** RC (grocer) (Kathleen Donaghey, George McLaughlin and Sadie Browne)

Newbuildings Street

1950 **John Browne Margaret Brown** (Kathleen Crumley), **Jimmy Browne,** (John Mitchell and Sadie Browne)

Quay Lane

1958 **Bridie Gillespie** (widow)

Foyle Crescent

1948-**50 Violet Curry** (Charlotte Temple)

1954 **Sadie Browne** RC **Margaret Cassidy** RC (fisherman) - the Cassidy family moved to Foyle Crescent in 1954 from Dam Row

1955 **Gerry Kelly** RC (fisherman) - (Sadie Browne)

1954-**63 Veronica McDaid** RC (bus driver) (John Mitchell and Sadie Browne) the McDaid family had moved from Kittybane

1955 **Martin Kelly**

1956 **Ann Kelly, Daniel (Danny) Browne**

1957 **Benny (Brendan?) Kelly, Margaret McDaid**

1958 **Michael Kelly, Daniel (Danny) Ferry, Gerard (Gerry) Browne**

1959 **John Ferry, Sarah (Sadie) Kelly, Mary McDaid**

Tully Bridge, Rossnagalliagh

1950 **Annie McClelland** P (labourer) came from Groarty Sch into 4th year on 18th Sept 1950 **Mabel Mc Clelland** P (labourer) came from Groarty Sch into Infants on 18th Sept 1950 **Evelyn McClelland** P (labourer) came on 18th Sept 1950 and left in 1955 to go to Newbuildings P Sch **Margaret Mary Park** C of I (cleaner in Sailors Rest) came on 6th Nov 1950 from Molenan Sch into 4th year **David Park**

1951 **Elizabeth Arthur** C of I (labourer) came on 11th Sept 1951 from Greerstown Sch into Infants **Doris Arthur** C of I (labourer) came on 11th Sept 1951 from Greerstown Sch and went into 1st year **Robert Arthur** C of I **Stewart Arthur** C of I **Jean Arthur** C of I

1952 **William McClelland** P (labourer), **Thomas McClelland** P (labourer), **Betty McClelland** P (labourer), **Nancy McClelland** P (labourer), **David McClelland** P (labourer)

1954 **John King RC, Arnold McClelland** P (labourer), went to Newbuildings P Sch in 1955

Kittybane

1951 **Mervyn Whiteside** P (bus driver)

Half mile Hill later Woodside Road

1954 **Marie Gillespie** RC, **Gerald Gillespie** RC, (John Mitchell and Sadie Browne)

1957 **James Gillespie**

1958 **Paul (Angus) Gillespie**

1959 **Patrick Flanaghan** (farmer)

Crocketts Hill, Kittybane

1955 **Mary McNamee** RC (Construction worker in England)

1957 **Terence McNamee, Deirdre McNamee**

Prehen

1950 **George (Ordie) Phillips** RC, **May Phillips** RC

1951 **James Phillips** RC

1954 **Patrick (Paddy) Phillips** RC, (Margaret Cassidy and Sadie Browne)

1955 **Anne McGonigle**

1958 **Adrian McGonigle, Eamon Burke, Eddie Phillips**

Cullion, Co Tyrone

Eileen Boyle, Danny Boyle, Patsy Boyle RC, (S Browne)

1959 **Patricia Boyle, Noel Boyle** – the Boyle family had previously attended Sandville School in Co Tyrone and stayed at Rossnagalliagh for a few years-also Marion Boyle? – their father may have worked as a roadman for the Council.

Burndennet

1944-50 **Ian Monroe** RC – past pupils recalled he came from Burndennet with Mrs McColgan. His mother may have come back from Canada, where her husband had been killed, to Burndennet where she had grown up. Ian was to do the 11+ examination in Rossnagalliagh and went on to St Columb's College. He may have returned to Canada.

Newbuildings Street

1950 **Florence McCracken** P (signal man) came on 29th May 1950

1948-50 **Robert Millar, Noel Miller, Keith Miller, John Millar, Eamon Millar, Gwen Millar, Teresa Miller,** (George McLaughlin and Charlotte Temple) – Millar family moved from Drumagor to Newbuidlings. The children attended Rossnagalliagh for a short period

The pupils attending in 1960-69

The number of children from Prehen increased in this period but fell from the Newbuildings area due to the opening of Newbuildings Primary School. Two children were to leave during the year,1964-65, and attended Waterside Boys School and Altnagelvin Special School.

Foyle Crescent (John Mitchell, George McLaughlin Bridgeen Rutherford)

1962 **Jeremiah Kelly, James Edward, P Kelly, Robert (Roy) Kelly,**

1963 **Bernadette Ferry**

1964 **Sarah Bernadette Brennan**

1965 **Kathleen Majella Brennan**

1966 **Maureen Elizabeth Ferry, Robert James McDaid** (bus driver), **E M Ann Phillips, John Henry Brennan** (p2)

1967 **M Patricia, E Phillips,** (p2) **William Kelly,** (p3) **Teresa Kelly**

1968 **K Bernadette Phillips, Ursula Mary Ferry**

1969 **John J Anthony Phillips, Margaret Mary (Margo) Brennan,** (p2) **Martin E Ferry**

Prehen (George McLaughlin)

1960 **Mary McDaid**

1962 **Imelda Connolly, Lorna Nangle** (bank manager)

1963 **Deidre Mary McCartie,** (doctor) **James (Jimmy) Nangle, Martin P Burke, James Doherty**

1964 **S Paul, Gregory O'Doherty,** (teacher) **Michael Martin O'Doherty,** (teacher) **Gerard Luke Nangle,** (bank manager) **Hugh Edward, Terence Gallagher, Anthony Bell, Janice M Cooley**

1965 **Peter Michael John Connolly, Andrew Donald Watts, Caroline Agnes McCloskey**

1966 **Rosemary Helen Campbell, Fiona Cooley, Mark Joseph O'Doherty, Barry Martin Nangle** (bank manager)

1968 **Angela Campbell, Nuala A Hegarty,** (p2) **John L C Connolly,** (p2) **Ciaran St John McCartie,** (doctor) **Ann Marie McFeely, Fiona J Nangle,** (bank manager) **Donna McCloskey**

1969 **Dermot J Hegarty, Grainne P Cooley, Grainne Catherine McCartie,** (p2) (doctor) **Ian E Watts, John Henry (Jackie) McFeely**

(Half Mile Hill- later Woodside Road)

1962 **John Gillespie** - Gillespie family lived at bottom of Woodside Road **Janice McNamee**

1963 **Sean Flanagan** (farmer)

1964 **Michael Richard Flanagan,** (farmer) **Kevin Joseph Foley,** (car breakers) The Foley family later moved to Donemana/Dunamanagh Road) **K Claire McNamee**

1965 **Margaret Ann Flanagan,** (farmer) **Dermot Foley, Ann Elizabeth Foley**

1967 **Geraldine Mary Flanagan** (farmer)

1969 **Pauline Bernadette Flanagan** (farmer)

Rossnagalliagh (Bridgeen Rutherford)

1964 **Bridgeen Mary O'Kane** (farmer) the O'Kane children were to attend Strabane Convent Primary School from 1969/70

1965 **Mary O'Kane** (farmer)

1966 **Michael Thomas O'Kane,**

1968 **John E O'Kane,** (farmer)

Hillhead, Rossnagalliagh

1964 **Elizabeth Ann Toland** (later Primity Crescent)

Hillview Av Prehen (George McLaughlin)

1965 **Catherine O'Flanaghan**

1966 **Paul Gerard King, Sean Patrick Gallagher**

1969 **Deidre Anne O'Flanaghan, Michael Gerard O'Flanaghan**

Victoria Road (previously known as Newbuildings Street)

1966 **John Paul Kerr**

1968 **Peter M Villa,** (publican) (p5) **Damian Villa** (publican) (P3)

1969 **Ronald F Villa** (publican)

Addresses unavailable for those below

1962 **Teresa Rogers**

1963 **Margaret E McGuire, Dermot Neil Alexander Peterson**

1964 Martin R Watts

1965 **Michael John Healy, Katherine Mary Quinn, Mary Patricia Traynor, Steven Gary Bulford,** (p2) **Peter Timothy Bulford**

1966 **Jacqueline Ann McKevitt, Marie Deirdre Bonner, Paul Martin Turner, Jacqueline Mary Turner, Lucille Rebecca Turner, Paul Anthony Healy, David Bulford, Karen Mary Jackson**

1967 **Andrew Ignatious O'Sullivan** (p3)

1969 **Paul D Kelly, James Gerald McDermott, Michael North**

Pupils attending from 1970-1977

New addresses in Newbuildings due to the building of social housing included Primity Crescent and Primity Terrace and private housing in Silverbrook. In addition to those already named, Catherine Kincaid and past pupils Siobhan Kenelly and Sinead Robb also helped with addresses in this period.

Newbuildings

1974 **Hugh Columba, Damian Wilson**

1976 **Gavin David Murray**

Primity Crescent

1971 **Elaine Carlin**

1972 **Barry Martin Carlin, Paul Anthony Latimer, Michael C McBride, Deborah A McAllister,** (p7) **Stephen A McAllister,** (p7) **Linda Carlin** (p3)

1973 Pauline Carlin, Donna Gillespie, Stephen Latimer, James McAllister, Dominic Joseph Dunne

1974 Mary Margaret Gillespie, John Edward McBride, Sinead M Robb, Patrick Francis Gillespie

1975 Tracey L Cooke, Kieran Patrick Gillespie, Dermot James O'Brien, (p2) Sheena Ann Robb, James McCallister (p2)

1976 Roisin Veronica Cooke, Gareth Martin Bonner, John Patrick Kay, Michael Christopher Kay, Anita Marie McBride

1977 Julie Anne Carlin, Stuart M Gillespie, Kathy Teresa McBride, Lisa M Robb

Primity Terrace

1970 Wendy B Williams

1971 Shirley Ann Williams, Stephen Joseph Doherty, Siobhan Doherty, Siobhan Mary Kennelly, Charles Smith, (p5) Robert Smith, Anna Marie Clancy, Teresa Frances Devine, Anthony Devine, (p2) Barbara Devine

1972 Marie Therese Mohamat, Jacqueline Williams, Eugene Arnett, Helen J Arnett, Brenda Claire Arnett, Catherine M Callan

1973 Kevin Doherty, Damian Martin Doherty

1974 Elizabeth May Williams, Carmel Fitzpatrick, Michelle Callan, Martin Joseph Devine

1975 Elizabeth Catherine Mohamet, Mark Doherty, Patrick Fox, (p3) Ursula E Kennelly, Gerard Francis Clancy, Patricia Clancy, (p3) Columba Matthew Callan, Patrick Andrew Callan

1976 Stephen Anthony Lewis Williams, Nuala Frances Doherty, Liam Gerard Doherty, Raymond Francis Doherty, Deborah Sharkey, (p4) Caroline Sharkey, (p2) Linda Sharkey, (p3) Julie Sharkey, (p7) Donna Nicola Smith, Joanne Smith Mary Teresa Fox, Richard Gerald Callan, Deborah Mary Callan

1977 Martina Sharkey (p5) Julie Marie Smith, Gareth Doherty, Kieran Patrick Doherty, Jacqueline Clancy

Foyle Crescent

1971 **Brian D Ferry**

1972 **Colm Patrick Ferry, Kathleen Ann Brown, Linda Brown, Mary Teresa (Maresa) Gormley, (p7) Geraldine Gormley, (p5) Siobhan Gormley, Christine Brown, Charlotte Brennan (p5)**

1973 **John Byrant (p2)**

1975 **Anne M Ferry, Rory McNamee**

1976 **Sinead Elizabeth Gormley, Patrick Kelly, Claire Catherine Ferry (p4)**

Prehen

1970 **Joseph Patrick Campbell, William Kieran Hegarty, Natalie Mailey (p2) Claire Dolores Gallagher, (p6) Maria A Blanking (p2)**

1971 Siobhan Michelle McFeely, Mary Bernadette McCay, (p7) Margaret McCay, (p2) Nuala Ann McCay, (p3) Sindy Jane Coyle, (P3) Kathleen Ann Harkin, Patricia F Harkin, Paul Gerard Morrison, Brian Morrison, Ann Bernadette McCauley, Martin Michael McCloskey, Paula McShane, Linda Mary McShane, Jacqueline Majella Connolly, Sean Terence Connolly, Owen Francis Blanking, (p5) Peter Hugh McDaid (p4)

1972 Fergal Hegarty, Amanda E Moore, Edward G McCay, Nuala McDaid, Conal Gallagher, Vincent Ambrose Kelly, Deirdre Kerr, Catriona Mullen, Desmond John McEnaney, Robert A (Tony) McGilloway, Joanna Blanking, Paul John O'Brien, (p6) Florence Mairead O'Brien

1973 Michael McFeely, Graham Watts, Gary Watts (Graham and Gary were twins), Paul McDaid, Damien Ward, Maria Harkin, Susan Morrison, Amanda McGilloway, Sharon O'Brien, Stephen Pulis, Cathal Ward (p7)

1974 Bronagh M Hegarty, C Tara Hegarty, (Bronagh and Tara were twins) Stephen McDaid, Clare Ward, (p4) Mary McMonagle, Lawrence McMonagle, (p3) Carmel (Carmela) Mc Monagle, (p2) Fiona E Mullan, Katherine L Mc Cauley, Eamon McLaughlin, Patrick M Kerr, (chef) Adrian Kerr, Paula Magee, Colum Mullan, Grainne Mullan, Gillian Denise McKeever, Dermot James O'Brien, Carmel E Gallagher (p5)

1975 Charles E McMonagle, Patrick Daniel Kell, Michael Hurley, (p7) Tracey Ann Pulis, Mark Sherrard, Natalie Mailey, (p2) Kevin Anthony Kelly (p4)

1976 Daniel Lawrence McFeely, Julie Ann Sherrard, (caravan salesman) Declan T Mc Laughlin, (p4) Daniel Harley, Fiona Mary Kell, (p2) Paul Gerard Kerr, Gavin David Murray, (p4) Joanne Harley, (p4) Joanne McAnerney, (p4) Damien Patrick McNulty, Emma Bell, (p2) Raymond Courtney, (p6) Sean Courtney (p7)

1977 Niamh McElholm

Half Mile Hill or Woodside Road

1972 Mary Cecilia Cassidy

1974 Mark Cassidy

1976 Deirdre Cassidy, Noel Brendan Flanaghan

1970 Eamon Christopher Flanagan (farmer)

1971 Kevin Martin Flanagan (farmer)

1974 Seamus Flanagan,(farmer)

1976 Noel Brendan Flanagan, (farmer) Arthur Dolan (p6)

Silverbrook

1970 Siobhan Karen McDermott

1972 Gareth Peter McGleenon, Lawrence McGonagle, Michael McLaughlin, M P Martin McGleenon (p3)

1974 Elaine Frazer

1976 Joan Frances Frazer, Brendan Frazer (p3)

1977 Siobhan Grant

Hillview, Prehen

1970 Helen Teresa O'Flanaghan, Michael Gerard O'Flanaghan, (p2) John Patrick King

1971 Deirdre Anne O'Flanaghan, (p4) , Patricia O'Flanaghan

1974 Peter Damian King, Marie Gallagher

Ballyorr Drive

1970, Isobel Sewell, Kevin A Dunne, (p2) Michael S Dunne (p5)

1971 Kevin Sala Reilly, James MP Sewell , Linda Sewell

1972 Donna M J Sievers, Florian Max Sperr, Brenda Elizabeth Stewart, Michael Earnest Joseph Tracey, Deidre E Tracey, Liam S Dunne

1973 Siobhan O'Donnell

1974 D Jude O'Donnell, Mark J O'Donnell, (p3) (children of Principal) Stewart Towns (p3)

1976 Katherine Quigley

Rossnagalliagh

1975 Aibhne C N O'Kane (farmer)

Victoria Road (previously Newbuildings Street)

1974 Mark Waldron (p3)

1975 Terence John Villa, (publican)Karen Ann Waldron

Addresses unavailable for those below

1971 Patricia Carmel O'Kane (p5)

1972 Paul Cullen (p5)

1974 Veronica Geraghty, (p6) Ian Stewart, (p5) Catherine Agnes Stewart, (p5)

1975 Sean Kelly

1976 Ciaran Patrick Kelly

1977 Lisa Maria Johnston, James Johnston, Marie Deirdre Bulford, Theresa McDaid

Appendix ii

Visitors to the school

Below is a list of some of the visitors to Rossnagalliagh School from 1915 to 1945 which were included in the Roll Books and Daily Report Books available. (-some names were difficult to decipher so may differ from those given.) The comments recorded by the visitors showed a positive view of school life.

The visitors included the Presbyterian clergy from Magheramason, some of whom sent their children to be educated at Rossnagalliagh. We have no record of the Rev. Caskey (1896-1908) visiting the school, but we can assume he did as his children attended the school. There is no record of Church of Ireland or Methodist clergy visiting.

The Roman Catholic clergy were regular visitors – Manager-Rev C McFaul, Rev D Quigley, 1914 -Rev P Kelly 1915 -Rev J Devlin 1916-37 manager Rev W B Mc Feely, Rev James Mc Glynn, 1916-27 -Rev Hugh Browne, -administrator of St Eugene's Cathedral, Rev D Kelly (Revs Kelly and Browne were from the local area)1916 - Rev Hugh McGlynn St Eugene' Cathedral, 1927 - Rev Mc Faul 1939- Rev James Mc Glynn, Waterside 1938-48 manager -Rev J L Mc Gettigan 1938-Rev B A Smith

1915-21st October-Rev Devlin found 38 pupils present and stated that the low number was due to a Station being in the district

1916 January 24th- Rev G D Erskine- Magheramason Presbyterian minister- he found work being carefully carried on;10th Nov W Mac Millan, District Inspector, visited from 9.50-10.10a.m. 19th December - Rev Gordon D Erskine found 56 pupils present and commented "much pleased with all that I saw"

1917 W Mc Millan, District Inspector, stayed from 2.40-3.00p.m. but only 37 out of 78 pupils were present

1918 9th April- Rev W Elliott reported that everything was in good order (this may have been a relative of Mrs Elliott, principal)

1923 20th June Rev P Kelly and Rev McFeely 7th August Rev McFeely visited 2.30.p.m.-3.00pm. 18th October Rev P Kelly and 19th October- Rev McFeely 22nd November – J S Mahon

1924 8th October J Mahon 3rd November Rev P Kelly

1925 J S Mahon

1927 12th January- Rev H C Browne

1930- 23rd October Dr Rev F W C Wallace, minister of Magheramason Presbyterian Church

1933- R J Colhoun and Mary Colhoun

1934 5th January Mr J Getty found everything in good order 9th March Revs James McGlynn and Rev Hugh Browne, 20th June- Mr Wm Colquhoun and R J Colquhoun

1935 15th January Mr A J Tuay

1936 Rev P Kelly recorded all was well

1937 7th May-Dr. Rev F W C Wallace

1938 31st October- Peader MacLoingsigh, St Columb's Waterside

1939- 4th December –Rev James McGlynn commented "all working hard"

1940 25th January- A J Donald remained from 1.00pm. to 3.00p.m. 22nd May J Phillip O'Connor of Ballymagorry, Strabane- commented "everything was satisfactory." On the same day AJ Donald returned and stayed from 1.15-3.00p.m.

1941. 18th November – Rev F.C.O'Hagan commented that all was "excellent"

1943 23rd June - N Stuart, of Magheracannon? stated that "Teachers and pupils very pleasing" 9th October -Squadron Leader (Rev) McShane, Royal Air Force, visited and commented that "Everything was going according to plan" (we are not told what plan he was alluding to!) Rev. Mc Shane may have come from the Waterside. A William Mc Shane had a shop in Spencer Road and may have been Rev McShane's brother. It is thought that Winifred Foley (nee Reid) who was a teacher in Rossnagalliagh, was also from Spencer Road and may have invited the Squadron Leader to visit the school. The visitor may also be a relative of McShanes of Bready.

1946 2nd July Squadron Leader (Rev) McShane, Royal Air Force visited once again. The end of WWII was celebrated with a sports day at Rossnagalliagh and this might have coincided with Rev McShane's visit.

Appendix iii

Holidays from School

While many of the children would not have gone away from home on holiday, nevertheless we can be sure that they looked forward to a break away from school life. Below are some of the annual and additional holidays for the years available in the Daily Report Books and Rolls. We can clearly see the respect given to both traditions throughout most of the life of the school in the "additional holiday" section. The school also closed due to many outbreaks of serious diseases.

Annual holidays

Church Holidays 1923 Ascension 10th May; Whit 25th May; Corpus Christi 31st May 1924 Good Friday 18th April St Patrick's Day, Easter –in 1924 22nd-25th April in 1933 there were six days holiday; in 1941 11-18th April; 1942 27th March-3rd April; 1959 27th March -3rdApril.

Summer holidays In 1914 31st July-14th September; 1918 mid August -end of September; 1920 3rd August-13th September;1923 13th August -21st September ; 1924 21st July - 29th August; 1925 4th August-11the September; 1927 28th July-1st September; 1934 1st August 24th August; 1936 9th July 21st August; 1937 26th July -1st September; 1941 21 July -1st September; 1947 11th August -5th September; 1958 15th July -29th August ; 1959 8th July -28th August

Christmas holidays 1919 23rd December -7th January; 1923 24th December -4th January; 1924 24th December -5th January; 1925 25th December- 1 st January; 1934 24th December – 31st December; 1941 24th December-6th January; 1958 24th December -6th January ; 1959 23rd December-5th January.

Potato gathering in 1940 an official holiday was given for the first time 1940 9th -18th October; 1942 12-23rd October; 1944-11-17th October; 1945 18th 23rd October; 1946-16th-18th October; 1947 7th 10th October.

Additional Holidays

1897 Royal anniversary- Queen Victoria's 60 th anniversary

191430th June Parochial excursion; 20th October-day given by the manager as there was a Station in the neighbourhood. An outbreak of Foot and Mouth affected cattle in the district but there is no record of the children getting a holiday from school due to the outbreak.

1915 Ascension Day; 1st March – day given by the manager for the children to attend the Station in the neighbourhood

1917 27th April Ecclesiastical examination; September-22nd October- closed due to an outbreak of scarlet fever

1923 3rd May-State holiday; 24th May- Empire Day; 9-20th July- closed due to influenza epidemic

1924 24th June Ecclesiastical Examination 24th October Station in the district

1925 Epidemic in the district-we are not told what the epidemic was but the children were off school for eight days; 18th June- Ecclesiastical examination 16th October-Station in the district

1927 25th March-Station day; 24th May -Empire Day

1928 24th May- Empire Day; 12th October –Royal visit to the area

1929 6-19th February-Influenza epidemic; 22nd February -11th March-Mr Donaghey, the school attendance officer, recorded that an epidemic of measles had followed the influenza epidemic; 29th March - vaccination of pupils

1933 30th November- Polling Day

1934 29th November- Royal wedding

1935 11th-28th July whooping cough epidemic also 2-16th September due to whooping cough epidemic

1936 28th January- King George V's funeral 12-14th May -Coronation of George VI

1936 2nd June-Polling day and 3rd June due to "cleaning up"

1937 8-9th March due to death of the schools manager; 12th -14th March- Blizzard;

1938 1-14th February-due to an unspecified epidemic; 23rd May -3rd June-scarlet fever epidemic ; 27th June -7th July scarlet fever epidemic 7th September –children absent due to mumps

1939 10th January- Funeral of Bishop Dr. Bernard O'Kane

1940 8-12 July -Evacuation of children

1941 14th February -3rd March-foot and mouth disease in the district

1942 26th February-20th March-measles epidemic

1945 29th January-2nd February –holiday due to "exceptional weather"(snow or frost) 8th-9th May -V E Days; 14th June Election (school used as an election booth); 12th July; 19th July -Royal visit of George V1 and Queen Elizabeth to Londonderry 17th October –death of Cardinal McRory

1947 18-27 February inclement weather (snow or frost) 23rd April –Royal visit to the area; 20th November-wedding of Princess Elizabeth and Prince Phillip

1948 26th April half day for the Royal Anniversary

1964 4th December 11+ verbal reasoning test

1965 15th January 11+ verbal reasoning test.

1970 January 14th –Teachers withdrew their labour

Appendix iv

Index of Proper Names